Fly Fishing Georgia

A No Nonsense Guide to Top Waters

David Cannon

Photography by Chad McClure
Foreword by Jimmy Harris

David Cannon fishes the trophy section of Dukes Creek.

NO NONSENSE

Tucson, Arizona

Fly Fishing Georgia
A No Nonsense Guide to Top Waters

ISBN-10 1-892469-20-0
ISBN-13 978-1-892469-20-5

© 2009 David Cannon and Charles McClure

Published by:
No Nonsense Fly Fishing Guidebooks
P.O. Box 91858
Tucson, AZ 85752-1858
(520) 547-2462
nononsenseguides.com

Printed in China

Editor: Howard Fisher

Maps, Knot Illustrations and Fly Photos:
    Pete Chadwell, Dynamic Arts

Photos: by Chad McClure, except where
    noted.

Design and Production: Doug Goewey

Front Cover: Drifting the Toccoa River.
    Photo by Chad McClure.

Back Cover: Jimmy Harris casting on the
    Chattooga River. Photo by
    David Cannon.

The No Nonsense Creed

The best way to go fly fishing is to find out a little something about a water, then just go there. Experimentation, trial-and-error, wrong turns, surprises, self-reliance, and new discoveries, even in familiar waters, are what make the memories. The next best way is to learn enough from a local to save you from going too far wrong. You still find the water on your own, and it still feels as if you were the first to do so.

This is the idea for our unique No Nonsense fly fishing series. Our books reveal little hush-hush information, yet they give all you need to find what will become your own secret places.

Painstakingly pared down, our writing is elegantly simple. Each title offers a local fly fishing expert's candid tour of his or her favorite fly fishing waters. Nothing is oversold or out of proportion. Everything is authentic, especially the discoveries and experiences you get after using our books. In his outstanding book *Jerusalem Creek*, Ted Leeson echoes our idea: "Discovering a new trout stream is a wonderful thing, and even if its whereabouts are common knowledge, to come upon the place yourself for the first time is nonetheless true discovery."

Art by Patsy Lewis-Gentry.

Where No Nonsense Guides Come From

No Nonsense guidebooks give you a quick, clear understanding of the essential information needed to fly fish a region's most outstanding waters. The authors are highly experienced and qualified local fly fishers. Maps are tidy versions of the author's sketches. These guides are produced by the fly fishers, their friends, and spouses of fly fishers, at No Nonsense Fly Fishing Guidebooks.

All who produce No Nonsense guides believe in providing top quality products at a reasonable price. We also believe all information should be verified. We never hesitate to go out, fly rod in hand, to verify the facts and figures that appear in the pages of these guides. The staff is committed to this research. It's hard work, but we're glad to do it for you.

Guide Kyle Burrell casts to a Chattahoochee
tailwater trout. Photo by David Cannon.

Table of Contents

Photo by David Cannon.

Photo by Joel Daniel.

Photo by David Cannon.

Photo by David Cannon.

Photo by David Cannon.

Photo by David Cannon.

David Cannon with a 16-pound striped bass from Lake Sidney Lanier. Photo by Henry Cowen.

About the Author

David Cannon caught his first fish at the age of five in his grandparents' pond on their farm in the Ozark Mountains of northwestern Arkansas. Little did he know then that a small bream caught on a bare hook would hatch a lifelong passion—some might even call it an obsession—in the pursuits of all things finned.

Growing up in the suburbs of north Atlanta, David could be found either on a basketball court or on the banks of a farm pond within a short walk of home. After heading into the mountains for college—first at Young Harris College, then at North Georgia College and State University—he discovered a strange fish in the local creeks that spent its entire life battling current all for the pleasure of eating a few small bugs. Not long after this discovery, David made another find—the fly rod—and he soon found himself in the vicious throws of addiction.

After spending a few months as an intern for Governor Sonny Perdue, he landed a job at the state's largest hunting and fishing magazine, *Georgia Outdoor News*. Because of his addiction, he was given the opportunity to write and was blessed with his own monthly column on fly fishing north Georgia called "Cannon's Creel," in addition to some news and feature writing.

In 2007, David jumped at the chance to work for Morris Sporting Group, publisher of *American Angler, Fly Tyer,* and the legendary *Gray's Sporting Journal.* While there, he worked in the advertising side of the business and wrote the "Closer Look" feature in *American Angler,* book reviews, and news briefs.

A member of the Georgia Outdoor Writers Association, David's words and photographs appear regularly in *American Angler, Georgia Sportsman, Georgia Outdoor News,* and *Alabama Outdoor News.* He is the Outdoor Editor for the *Athens Banner-Herald* newspaper. One of his photos appeared on the cover of Brian O'Keefe's and Todd Moen's outstanding online journal of fly fishing photography and video, *Catch Magazine.*

He and his wife Stephanie live east of Atlanta and are members of First Baptist Church Loganville, the Rabun Chapter of Trout Unlimited, and the Atlanta Fly Fishing Club. When not fishing, writing, or shooting photos, David enjoys speaking to fly fishing clubs, watching Texas Longhorn football with his father, building furniture and woodturning, and searching for the world's best barbecue with his wife.

To learn more and view additional outdoor photos and video, see CannonOutdoors.com.

Chad McClure gets ready to fish a mountain stream. Photo by Pam McClure.

About the Photographer

For Chad McClure, two boyhood hobbies have developed into lifelong passions. The Augusta native picked up his first camera as an eight-year-old and has been documenting the world around him ever since. He has also been fishing for as long as he can remember and first discovered the sport of fly-fishing as a teenager.

As an avid outdoorsman, Chad has been hunting and fishing the woods and waters of the southeast most of his life. He finds as much pleasure in fishing sixty miles off the coast as in the small streams of northern Georgia. A graduate of the University of Georgia's Grady College of Journalism, Chad began his photography career at the *Chattanooga Times Free Press,* where he honed his skills as a staff photojournalist under the guidance of editor Billy Weeks.

He continues to do freelance photography and has been published in magazines including *Gray's Sporting Journal, American Angler, Stratos, Georgia Sportsman, Georgia Outdoor News,* and *Western Horseman.* His photos also grace books, including *Tennessee 24/7* and *The Best Fly Fishing in the Southeast,* as well as many daily newspapers.

Chad is employed by Morris Sporting Group where he works on *Gray's Sporting Journal, American Angler,* and *Fly Tyer.* When not fishing, he enjoys hunting, wingshooting, and gardening. Chad and his wife, Pam, live in Thomson, Georgia, with their wonderful dogs. See chadmcclure.com.

Dedications

This book is dedicated to four important people in my life:

To my wife, Stephanie.
You're my first, my last, my everything, and I couldn't have completed this book without you.
I hope this book makes you proud.

To my parents, Jay and Mary Cannon.
Thank you for the ridiculous amounts of love and encouragement you've always thrown my way.
I hope this book makes you proud.

To my friend and fly-fishing mentor, Jeff Durniak.
Thank you for being sympathetic and taking the time to help the guy in the Smithgall Woods parking lot who got skunked. Your instruction has saved me years of frustration.
I hope this book makes you proud.

—David Cannon

I would like to give special thanks to my wife, who supports me in all that I do.
I would also like to thank my parents for their love and patience.

—Chad McClure

Releasing a Brown by Bucky Bowles.

Acknowledgments

Before I acknowledge all of the amazing people who offered their expertise to make this book a great resource, I think I'd be remiss to be able to spend so much time in Creation without at least acknowledging the Creator. We are blessed to live in an area rich with natural beauty and life. It's difficult for me to witness all of this and not see a loving Creator behind it all.

It would not be possible to write a book on fly fishing Georgia without the help of many people, especially Jimmy Harris of Unicoi Outfitters; renowned fly designer, writer, guide, and friend to everyone, Henry Cowen; and of course, the Georgia Department of Natural Resources.

Covering our cold-water fisheries, I owe a big thank you to Chris Scalley and Kyle Burrell at River Through Atlanta guide service, as well as Don Pfitzer for their help on the incredible Chattahoochee tailwater. Chris's knowledge of the river is staggering and I'd put Kyle with fly-rod-in-hand up against the tag-team duo of an electro-fishing Department of Natural Resources biologist and a blue heron any day of the week. It was also great having access to the knowledge of David Hulsey and Julian Byrd on the streams surrounding the town of Blue Ridge, as well as great fishing author and *Georgia Sportsman* editor Jimmy Jacobs. Also thanks to Jimmy Harris and Jeff Durniak on the Chattooga River and Richie Santiago and Carter Morris on Waters Creek. And I would also like to acknowledge Rex Gudgel for helping out with many of the private waters, for helping me become a better fly-caster, and for being insanely quick with a net!

Across Georgia's warm waters, thanks to Kent Edmonds for his assistance at Callaway Gardens and for sharing his knowledge of the Flint, perhaps Georgia's most unique river. I also appreciate Cody Jones for his help at Barnsley Gardens and on the Savannah River, the knowledge of Mike Floyd and Jeremy Altman, owner of Buckeye Lures. Thanks to Jeff Gillespie and Mark Ellis for pointing me to Bull Sluice Lake and sharing their expertise on the most challenging of freshwater fish, the carp. A special thanks goes to Bill Howle on Clarks Hill Reservoir, Buddy Lail on Lake Varner, Nathan Lewis on Blue Ridge Reservoir, and Mike Sloan on Lake Seminole.

On the coast, I really appreciate the help of Greg Hildreth, Larry Kennedy, and Scott Owens. Also, thanks to Thornton Morris and Paul Puckett for putting us up while on the surreal Cumberland Island.

I am grateful to four great sporting artists—Paul Puckett, Bucky Bowles, Patsy Lewis-Gentry, and the late Tom Landreth (a special thanks to June Landreth)—for allowing their beautiful artwork to appear in this work.

Paul Puckett is to be recognized for specially creating his wonderful pencil sketches of the flies featured for each water.

I would also like to recognize Steve Walburn, editor of *American Angler* and general manager of the Morris Sporting Group, and O. Victor Miller who have both inspired me through their incredible writing. To Daryl Kirby, who gave me my first column in *Georgia Outdoor News,* Russ Lumpkin, Nick Carter, and Brad Gill, thanks for teaching me about good story writing. Thanks to Chad McClure, Brian O'Keefe, and Lefty Kreh for being patient in answering each of my thousands of photography questions. And I wouldn't have had the privilege of working in this great industry if not for the graces of Steve Burch, Mike Rhodes, and one of the greatest outdoor writers in Georgia's history, Brad Bailey, all of *Georgia Outdoor News.*

Of course, what would fishing be without the company of good fishing buddies? To Andy Spencer, Matt Anderson, Mark Musselwhite, Ryan Whitelaw, Daniel Brown, and Bear Keeling, thanks for those times on the water and for consistently asking me questions like, "You write magazine articles on this stuff?" and the latest, "You're writing a book about this?" I greatly value your willingness to keep me humble when I lose a fish, miss a hook-set or, on occasion, fish without even tying on a fly.

I'd especially like to acknowledge Howard Fisher and all of the great people at No Nonsense Guidebooks for allowing me to work on this project, and Brian and Jenny Grossenbacher—authors of *Fly Fishing Montana*—for introducing me to Howard Fisher. Morenci Clark, Anthony Taylor, Lori Brown, and Howard have been phenomenal to work with and have made this process a great one for me.

Finally, thanks to my wife Stephanie, and Joel and Hilary Mulkey for proofing the drafts of the book, and to Uncle "Foo" (Steve Thulis), my cousin Greg Thulis, and my dad Jay Cannon for getting me interested in fishing. I'm not sure what I'd be doing had I not been introduced to this wonderful world.

The author nymphs a run on a mountain trout stream.

Foreword

By Jimmy Harris

When I met David several years ago, I quickly took a liking to him. He was doing all he could to become a better fly fisherman. David was like a sponge, soaking up every tidbit of information anyone tossed his way. He fished with anyone who would let him tag along, often standing off to the side watching as they successfully worked a run that he or another angler may have just fished with no luck. Always doggedly chasing the desire to know more, he arranged for advanced casting lessons with certified instructors, fished for every species that swims from the mountains to the coast of Georgia, and even traveled out of the country to pursue this passion.

Along the way, he also discovered a love and talent for writing about our sport, our quarry, and those who have been captured by its mystique. True to his nature, he has spent the past few years relentlessly developing this talent and, for that, we should all be grateful. And just as he shadowed more experienced anglers, David has tapped into many of the most respected angling journalists, photographers, editors and publishers to help him hone his craft. Lefty Kreh, James Babb, Brian O'Keefe, and others have all given their personal attention to his professional growth and it is evident in this book.

Most anglers from outside the state undoubtedly associate Georgia with world-class bass fishing. However, Georgians have known for a long time that fishing opportunities here, and particularly fly fishing opportunities, are boundless. From the southernmost reaches of the Appalachian Mountains to the Piedmont and Coastal Plains, we can fish every day of the year. From small rhododendron-choked wild trout streams to huge impounds where stripers and hybrid bass roam like packs of wolves in search of their next meal, we've got it all. Six species of black bass, bream, catfish, and carp swim in our piedmont and coastal plain rivers and farm ponds. Redfish, tarpon, sea trout, and sharks roam the estuaries and surf on the coast. For the fly fishing angler, there isn't a better state in the country for sheer abundance of opportunity. While more famous fly fishing regions of the country have brief seasons of great fishing interrupted by long months of reading about fishing and tying in preparation for next year, we're just changing rods and technique for another species.

Jimmy is the co-owner of Unicoi Outfitters, which operates a guide service and fly shops in the towns of Blue Ridge and Helen. He has appeared on several television shows including Fly Fishing America *and has fly-fished in Georgia for nearly four decades. Photo by David Cannon.*

And this is the value of David's book! With succinct yet easily read prose, *Fly Fishing Georgia: A No Nonsense Guide to Top Waters* opens up all the great opportunities awaiting you in our state. The inspiring photography by Chad McClure, David, and his beautiful wife Stephanie, along with the illustrations provided by renowned artists Bucky Bowles, Paul Puckett, Patsy Lewis-Gentry, and the late Tom Landreth have made this a book you'll want for the visual senses alone.

David has done a wonderful job of identifying Georgia's fly fishing resources and giving you, the reader, the information you'll need to pursue any of a myriad of species throughout the seasons. You'll want to keep this book handy for quick reference when you've just got to get out on the water or when you're planning your next extended fishing trip. I know I will.

Fly Fishing Georgia

Writing this book was a great experience for me personally. It was both educational and fun all along the way. So it only makes sense that my two main objectives while putting this book together were to first provide you, the reader, with enough information to help you attain some level of success at each location and second, to get you excited about fishing these spots and the state as a whole. After all, you can cast a fly to redfish along the Gulf Coast, to strong stripers in the Northeast, to lunker bass in Texas, or to beautiful trout out west. Or, you can buy one Georgia fishing license and pursue all of the above species throughout the course of one year in the Peach State.

In light of those two objectives, I burned the midnight oil many nights picking over and marking maps, learning the history and back stories of the locations, cross-referencing hatch charts with local accounts and

Jay Cannon battles on the delayed harvest section of the Toccoa River. Photo by David Cannon.

putting all of that together as clearly and concisely as I know how. I also fished—a lot—but that was mostly during the daytime. And because I am far from being an expert on any of the featured locations, I double-checked my information with Georgia's true experts—the experienced locals, the great guides who spend their lives on these waters, and some of the many wonderful people at the Georgia Department of Natural Resources.

How to Use This Book

This book was written for anglers, plain and simple, no matter at what experience level he or she may be. Everything in this book will be simple enough for any beginner and because this book covers coldwater, warmwater, and saltwater fisheries, it will even help the expert angler who has been fishing the Chattooga River for 50 years when he decides to take a trip to Georgia's Golden Isles.

Each featured location description provides enough information to get an angler on the path to success, including a clearly marked full-page map, fish forage that could be present, suggestions on flies to match that forage, recommendations for appropriate gear, and peak fishing times. Be sure to utilize the Resources section of the book for contact information of local fly shops and guides in the given areas.

Catch and Release

I don't mind an angler taking home a legal number of fish from heavily stocked sections of some of Georgia's trout streams. As one Georgia angler put it, "Stockers are like Doritos; the DNR can make more whenever they want." However, I would strongly discourage anyone from ever keeping a trout from a wild stream. I would also like to encourage anglers to release any "trophy" catches, no matter the species. If you really want a mount of your catch, or something like a catch and release painting by Georgia artist Paul Puckett, please know that most modern replicas use no part of the actual fish. So take a few photos and a length and girth measurement of your catch and then release the fish to fight another day. Another angler could be glad you did.

Rules and Regulations

Some of the regulations regarding trophy, artificial-only, or catch and release waters are mentioned within the text of their pertinent chapters. However, these regulations can change from year to year and it is your responsibility as an angler to be fully aware of any and

A beautiful 20-inch rainbow trout from Dukes Creek.

all governing rules and licensing needed to legally fish these waters. All of this information and more can be found at gofishgeorgia.com.

Conservation

In the heart of the Deep South, it is truly amazing that we can boast of more than 4,000 miles of trout streams in our state. Many of these waters are suitable for trout only through careful management and hard work to maintain sufficient habitat. So, by lending a hand with installing stream structures at a Trout Unlimited workday or by picking up someone else's trash while fishing, conservation is something in which we all can play a part.

Hazards and Safety

A safe day on the water begins before you leave your home. While it's easy to run out the door with nothing but your waders, boots, fly rod and vest, there are several items that are far more important for your safety.

For starters, take and drink plenty of water. If you must fish alone—and I highly recommend always fishing with a buddy—let someone know where you will be and what time you will return. Sunscreen should also be a major consideration for anglers, particularly those fishing on open water or high-elevation streams where there is less protection from UV rays. Anglers have a higher risk of developing skin cancers, particularly on the back of the neck and ears, so products that shield against UV-A and UV-B should be worn at all times while on the water.

Planning accordingly for clothing can really make or break a trip, too. Layering is a good idea and it's better to have too many layers as opposed to too few. On both ends of the spectrum, heat stroke or hypothermia can really sneak up on an intensely focused angler, but both can be avoided. And considering the moisture-wicking materials employed by many of the clothing manufacturers today, a safe day on the water can also be a pretty comfortable one. Of course, no fabric is good enough to wick the amount of moisture that comes along with taking a good dunking. So, keep a spare set of clothes in the car just in case.

Flashlights and extra batteries in a waterproof bag should be a mainstay in any fly angler's chest pack or vest. They are needed both in the instance of getting lost and, because some of the best fishing occurs in that magic hour leading up to dark, to aid in getting back to your vehicle.

Finally, anglers exploring moving waters should place top priority on safety while wading or floating. Moving water should never be underestimated or taken lightly. It is a powerful and potentially dangerous force. While wading, keep good contact with the river bottom at all times. Employing the use of a collapsible wading staff and a personal floatation device is a good idea, too. It's also best to stay within sight of another person in case help is needed. And especially while fishing tailwaters, like the Toccoa River downstream of Lake Blue Ridge or the Chattahoochee below Lake Sidney Lanier, it is imperative to know when the respective dams will be releasing water. Telephone numbers or Web sites that provide release schedules and flow information should be used every time you fish tailwaters.

Rods

A good rod can become a good friend over the years, but that doesn't mean it has to be expensive. There are few, if any, modern graphite rods that won't do the job and that don't come with a good warranty, an example of that being one of my favorites which cost a whopping $31. Fly rods

A big Toccoa tailwater rainbow is measured before being released. This fish, caught by WRD Fisheries Supervisor Jeff Durniak, was 21 inches long.

brine rinse your reel with plenty of freshwater, even if the manufacturer says the reel's inner workings are sealed.

Fly Line

If you are going to spend top dollar for any one fly fishing item, choose to spend it here. Even though it's called "fly fishing," you're actually casting the weighted fly line and the fly itself is just along for the ride. It's like saying, "I'm flying to Dallas tomorrow." You're not really flying—you're a passenger on a plane that's flying. It's the same story for the fly.

For most fishing applications, a floating weight-forward fly line will do the trick. However, if the fish are holding deeper in the water column, you can deliver your fly by using either an intermediate- or fast-sinking fly line, which are measured in grains instead of by weight—the higher the grain number, the faster the line will sink.

If you know you'll be fishing in very specific conditions, know that most fly line manufacturers now have different fly line tapers to match nearly any angling situation, like a short, heavy taper for turning over bushy bass flies or a longer, lighter taper for making long casts to spooky redfish.

Leaders

This is an important part of the equation, too. Tapered leaders made of either nylon- or fluorocarbon monofilament (nylon floats and fluoro sinks) aid in transferring the energy from the fly line to (hopefully) delicately turn over your fly upon delivery to the fish. When using floating fly lines, the leader will normally fall in the 7 ½ to 12-foot range with the most common length being 9 feet. While utilizing sinking fly lines, shorter leaders ranging from three to six feet should be used to help the angler detect strikes.

Tippet

If you purchase a brand new leader tapered to 5X, that means the last couple of feet of the leader will be the diameter of 5X. Until you clip off that length over the course of retying different flies to your leader, there is no need to attach tippet material of the same diameter to the leader, unless of course you see the need for a longer leader. Be sure to join tippets and leaders of like material—nylon mono to nylon mono and fluorocarbon to fluorocarbon. Fluorocarbon is much harder than nylon and can slice it when the pressure of a fighting fish is applied.

Clothing

While we've reviewed the importance of clothing with regards to safety, it can be noted that clothing for the fly angler is as important as camouflage for the hunter.

are classified by weight—the higher the rod weight, the heavier the fly line it will be able to cast effectively.

Trout and panfish rods are generally 0 to 5 weights and usually 8 to 9 feet long, though specialty rods can be as short as 5 feet for tight brookie streams or as long as 10 feet for fishing larger waters. Bass rods are generally 7 feet 11 inches to 9 feet long and come in weights 6 to 10, which allows them to cast bushy bass bugs. Rods for saltwater are usually 9 to 10 ½ feet long and go from an 8 weight for inshore fishing all the way up to a 15 weight for bluewater battles.

Reels

For panfish and any trout smaller than around 16 inches, the reel rarely comes into play aside from its line-holding function. However, if there is a chance of tangling with larger fish, whether in the salt or in freshwater, a reel with a good, dependable disc drag is a necessity. Keep in mind that in all but the most expensive reels, you'll have to choose between the standard- or mid-arbor reel or the higher retrieval rate of a large-arbor reel, which also offers more backing capacity. Any time you fish the

The fish we chase may have brains the size of a reel handle, but they still have instincts that tell them to swim away or stop feeding when they see a threat. So, another function of clothing while fishing is to keep you, the angler, out of sight.

Trout are used to their predators coming from above, so if you're fishing a mountain stream lined by rhododendron and mountain laurel, choose dark or even camo-colored clothing. If you're fishing open water in the salt or on a reservoir, try to blend in with the sky behind you. In many of the pictures throughout this book, the photo subject is wearing a bold or contrasting color, but that is only for aesthetics—do not wear a bright red sweater while fishing the Conasauga River!

Wading Gear

Larger rivers should be fished while wearing chest-high waders and smaller streams can typically be waded in hip- or waist-high waders during the cooler months. Warmer months call for wet-wading while wearing either shorts or quick drying pants and wading boots or sandals. Keep in mind that wading boots should always have soles made of either felt or another gripping material to assist in safely traversing slick rocks.

Hatches

Western rivers and Pennsylvania limestone spring creeks don't have a monopoly on good hatches—we have plenty here in Georgia, too. In fact, we even have mayfly hatches on our large reservoirs in the summer that reach Biblical proportions (mayflies are sometimes referred to as "willow bugs" on these lakes). The Known Hatches portion found in the sidebar of each location is based on information collected over the years by the real experts. There are three hatch charts featured throughout this book—one for freestone streams in Southern Appalachia, one specifically for the Chattahoochee River tailwater, and another based on the insects present on the Toccoa River tailwater. I'd like to especially thank Doug Adams of the Rabun Chapter of Trout Unlimited, Chris Scalley and his Chattahoochee Coldwater Fishery Foundation, and David Hulsey of Unicoi Outfitters, respectively, for assembling these charts and making them available for all of us.

Fly Patterns

One of the most daunting parts of entering the wonderful world of fly fishing is the vast number of different fly patterns. Luckily, the No Nonsense Guidebook format allows us the space to showcase color photos of many of the proven patterns. Of course, if you're a seasoned veteran in the fly fishing game, you already know what a Y2K Bug looks like. But I'm sure even the most expert among us will be excited to see the nationally-recognized patterns of a Brooklyn native that we Georgians have adopted as our own, Henry Cowen, and the flies the Chattahoochee tailwater trout can't turn down by Chris Scalley, and the awesome popping bugs and sliders by fellow Young Harris College alum Steve Davenport. I'm sure everyone will also be happy to see Kent Edmonds's warmwater flies, Rob Rooks's famed "Berry" series, and Mark Ellis's patterns for the wary carp.

One-man pontoons are great watercraft for fishing some of our more shallow rivers like the Toccoa. Photo by David Cannon.

Renowned Chattahoochee River guide Chris Scalley casts for wild brown trout just north of Atlanta. Photo by David Cannon.

Fly Shops

Seeing the smiling faces of Willie at Fly Box Outfitters in Kennesaw, John or Hamp at Unicoi Outfitters in Helen, David or Julian at the Unicoi shop in Blue Ridge, Mark at Highland Outfitters in Cartersville, or any of the characters at The Fish Hawk in Atlanta is to be expected like the caddis hatch on the 'Hooch. And while I hope this book becomes a trusted source for anglers across our state, it's the people working these shops who will be able to offer the best advice, whether on which rod to purchase or what flies are working. Do business with these folks as often as possible so they will stay in business, then we'll all continue to have a great resource for information.

Guides

I have done my best to locate and list reputable fly fishing guides who operate in Georgia in the Resources section. However, if anyone was omitted, that shouldn't be a reflection on their knowledge or ability to show a client a good day on the water. Many Georgia guides spend almost every day on the water, either with a client or just doing research. Most of us can definitely benefit from their knowledge. If you're new to fly fishing and can afford it, hire a guide as often as you can. If you're a competent angler and want to learn a new stream or lake, hire a guide. If you're competent and know the area, and want to add to your knowledge base and techniques, hire a guide.

Private Waters

Sometimes it's nice to get away from the crowds and head to private waters to chase large fish. This will cost a little money, but it's a great treat to visit any of the pay-to-fish waters listed in the Private Waters section. I recommend them all wholeheartedly.

Ratings

I rated each location in this book on a scale of 1-10 (poor to excellent). The ratings are found at the end of each sidebar and are completely subjective. Of course the enthusiasm of the rater is never in short supply.

Clubs and Organizations

Perhaps the best way for someone new to fly fishing to learn about the sport and good locations is to join a local chapter of Trout Unlimited, The Federation of Fly Fishers, or the Coastal Conservation Association. Apart from being great conduits for meeting new fishing buddies and pulling from others' knowledge, each of these organizations uses their dues and donations to protect and improve habitat for the survival of the fish we pursue. Also, groups like the Georgia Outdoor Network and the Georgia Wildlife Federation's Camo Coalition, which lobby for sportsmens' rights, are worth supporting to ensure that we have places to fish in the future and proper management of those places. Contact information for these organizations and local chapters can also be found in the Resources section.

Southern Appalachian Freestone Streams Hatch Chart

Courtesy of the Rabun Chapter of Trout Unlimited

Insect	Jan	Feb	Mar	April	May	June	July	Aug	Sept	Oct	Nov	Dec
Blue-Winged Olive	X	X	X							X	X	X
Midges	X	X	X							X	X	X
Winter Black Stonefly	X	X	X									
Small Dun Caddis		X	X									
Blue Quill Mayfly			X	X								
Quill Gordon Mayfly			X	X								
Early Black Stonefly			X	X								
Cream Caddis				X								
Red Quill				X	X							
March Brown Mayfly				X	X	X						
Yellow Stonefly					X	X	X					
Light Cahill Mayfly					X	X	X					
Speckled Gray Caddis					X	X						
Giant Black Stonefly					X	X						
Sulphur Mayfly					X	X						
Golden Stonefly						X	X					
Brown and Slate Drakes						X	X					
Green Drake Mayfly					X	X						
Coffin Fly/Green Drake Spinner					X	X						
Gray/Brown & Green Caddis						X	X	X	X			
Speckled Gray/Brown Caddis							X	X	X	X		
Brown Stonefly							X	X				
Trico Mayfly							X	X	X			
Terrestrials						X	X	X	X	X		
October Caddis									X	X	X	

Insect	Sizes	Dry Flies	Nymphs
Blue-Winged Olive	16–20	Blue-Winged Olive, Blue Quill, Adams Parachute	Blue-Winged Olive Nymph, Pheasant Tail Nymph
Midges	18–22	Griffith's Gnat	Midge Pupa, Brassie, Serendipity
Winter Black Stonefly	16–20	Black Elk Hair Caddis, Griffith's Gnat	Black Stonefly Nymph, Pheasant Tail Nymph
Small Dun Caddis	18	Brown Elk Hair Caddis	Hare's Ear Nymph
Blue Quill Mayfly	16–18	Blue-Winged Olive, Blue Quill, Adams Parachute	Blue-Winged Olive Nymph, Pheasant Tail Nymph
Quill Gordon Mayfly	12–14	Quill Gordon	Quill Gordon Nymph
Early Black Stonefly	16–18	Black Elk Hair Caddis, Griffith's Gnat	Black Stonefly Nymph, Pheasant Tail Nymph
Cream Caddis	12–14	Elk Hair Caddis	Dark Cream Caddis Pupa
Red Quill	14–16	Red Quill, Hendrickson	Pheasant Tail Nymph
March Brown Mayfly	12–14	March Brown, Adams Parachute	March Brown, Dark Hare's Ear, Pheasant Tail
Yellow Stonefly	14–16	Yellow Stimulator, Elk Hair Caddis (Yellow)	Yellow Stonefly Nymph
Light Cahill Mayfly	12–14	Light Cahill, Light Cahill Parachute	Light Cahill Nymph, Hare's Ear Nymph
Speckled Gray Caddis	12–14	Dark Elk Hair Caddis	Dun and Yellow/Brown Caddis Pupa, Hare's Ear
Giant Black Stonefly	4–8	None	Black Stonefly Nymph
Sulphur Mayfly	14–18	Sulphur Comparadun, Light Cahill, Cream Variant	Sulphur Nymph or Emerger, Pheasant Tail Nymph
Golden Stonefly	4–8	None	Golden Stonefly Nymph
Brown and Slate Drakes	8–14	Adams Parachute, Blue Dun Parachute, March Brown Parachute	March Brown Nymph, Dark Hare's Ear Nymph, Pheasant Tail Nymph
Green Drake Mayfly	8–10	Green Drake, Light Cahill Parachute	Green Drake Nymph
Coffin Fly/Green Drake Spinner	8–10	Spent Wing Coffin Fly, Parachute Coffin Fly	None
Gray/Brown & Green Caddis	14–16	Dark Elk Hair Caddis with Green	Dun and Green Caddis Pupa
Speckled Gray/Brown Caddis	14–16	Dark Elk Hair Caddis with Yellow/Brown	Dun and Yellow Caddis Pupa
Brown Stonefly	10–12	None	Brown Stonefly Nymph
Trico Mayfly	20–22	Parachute Trico, Poly Wing Spinner (Black)	None
Terrestrials	Various	Various	Various
October Caddis	8–10	Ginger Elk Hair Caddis	Ginger Caddis Pupa

Flies to Use in Georgia—Dries & Terrestrials

Adams Parachute

Adult Midge

Ant

Beetle

Black Foam Flying Ant

Blue-Winged Olive

Blue-Winged Olive Criple

Cannon's Abigail Adams

Chernobyl Ant, Cherry

Dave's Cricket

Dave's Hopper

Elk Hair Caddis

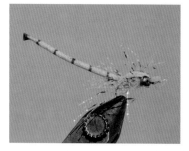
Foam Damsel

Goddard's Caddis

Griffith's Gnat

Hot Butt Caddis

Humpy

Light Cahill

Madam X

Quill Gordon

Royal Stimulator

Royal Trude

Royal Wulff

Scalley's Cripple Caddis

Schroeder's Parachute Hopper

Slow Water Caddis

Sofa Pillow

Stimulator

X Caddis

Yellow Sally

Nymphs

Barr's Copper John

Beadhead Zebra Midge

Brassie

Disco Midge

Hare's Ear

Kaufmann's Stone

Lightning Bug

Pheasant Tail

Prince Nymph

Rooks's Berry Nymph

Scalley's Miracle Nymph

Scud

Stonefly Nymph

WD-40

Zug Bug, Beadhead

Streamers and Wet Flies

Black Fur Ant

Conehead Bugger

Double Bunny

Glo Bug, Orange

Hornberg

Krystal Bugger

Mickey Finn

Muddler Minnow

San Juan Worm

Scalley's Bugsy Shad

Scalley's Electric Bugger

Turck's Tarantula

Woolhead Sculpin

Woolly Bugger

Zonker, Olive

Warmwater Flies

Braided Butt Damsel

Carter's Rubber-legged Dragon

Chuck's Claw-Dad, Brown

Clouser's Crayfish

Clouser's Deep Minnow

Dahlberg's Diver

DP Popper

DP Slider

Ellis's Bling Cray

Ellis's Hook-up Nymph

Kent's Stealth Bomber

Threadfin Shad

Walt's Frog Slider

Whitlock's Crayfish

Whitlock's Deer Hair Popper

Saltwater and Striper Flies

Blados's Crease Fly

Blanton's Flashtail Whistler

Blanton's Sar-Mul-Mac

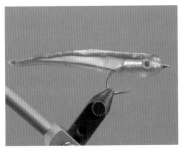

Chocklett's Gummy Minnow

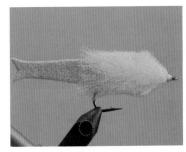

CK Baitfish, Chartreuse

Cowen's Baitfish

Cowen's Coyote

Cowen's Somethin' Else

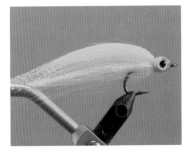

DuBiel's Lil Hadden

DuBiel's Red-Ducer, Tan

Hanley's Beach Ball

Lefty's Deceiver

Matthews's Bonefish Bitters

Russell's Mussel

Walt's Saltwater Popper, Chartreuse

David Cannon readies a nymphing rig for a deep run of the Tallulah River.

Top Georgia Fly Fishing Waters

Photo by Jimmy Harris.

Photos by David and Stephanie Cannon.

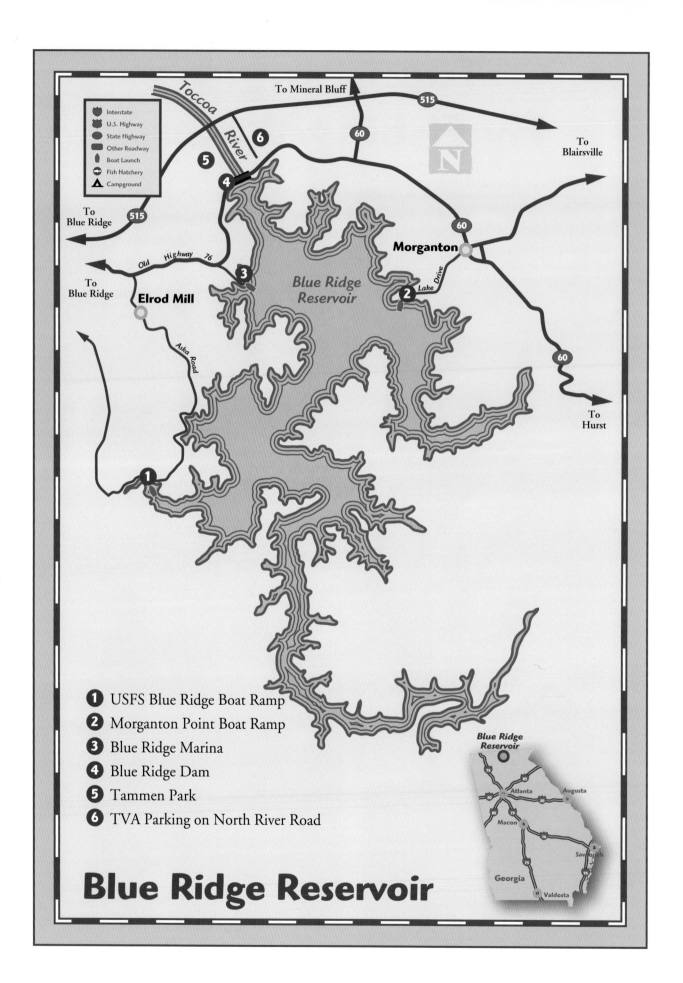

1 USFS Blue Ridge Boat Ramp

2 Morganton Point Boat Ramp

3 Blue Ridge Marina

4 Blue Ridge Dam

5 Tammen Park

6 TVA Parking on North River Road

Blue Ridge Reservoir

Blue Ridge Reservoir

Most fly anglers I know are happy people. And if opposites truly do attract, as the song suggests, maybe that would explain the fascination fly fishers have with the smallmouth bass. Smallies, it seems, are just plain angry. They are anger in finned form. I don't know what they're angry about, but put a hook in one of their faces and watch what happens. They go berserk. If you were to take a step back and watch an angler fight a smallmouth, you would literally witness the spectrum of emotion in physical form. On one end, we have the crazy, raging smallmouth. As the spectrum transfers from fish to the fisherperson, anger turns into pure euphoria as energy passes through fly then leader, line then rod, and nerves to human brain. Opposite the fish lies the opposite emotion. For the angrier they get during a fight, the happier the fly angler gets. And that probably makes smallies even more enraged. It's a vicious cycle.

Blue Ridge Reservoir by Blue Ridge, Georgia—with its deep, clear, and cold water over rocky underterrain—is now the only viable fishery for smallmouth in the entire state. It was opened for business in 1930 and is a polite 3,290-acre interruption in the

An angler works a cove from the banks of Blue Ridge.

Anglers Jimmy Harris (left) and Andy Spencer cast to Blue Ridge smallies.

Casting to rocky banks on Blue Ridge will usually produce a smallmouth.

Poppers, sliders and baitfish patterns are good to have on hand when targeting the feisty smallmouth bass.

Blados's Crease Fly

Toccoa River's journey northward to the Tennessee state line.

Fishing here for the hard-fighting smallmouth is best for fly rodders in April, May, October, and November when they are pushing blueback herring to the surface. This is no easy angling, though. While the smallies will strike nearly any surface fly quickly delivered and stripped through their area of attack, the challenge is getting the fly to them in time. Oftentimes, this surface action lasts for only a few seconds. Being able to quickly deliver a fly 50 feet or more is a necessary skill here.

When the fish aren't readily showing themselves, a little blind-casting is in order. This is when good electronics are essential. Using a fish finder, try to pattern where the fish are holding in the water column. Then, utilize an intermediate or full-sinking fly line depending upon their depth. Getting a Clouser Minnow, Lefty's Deceiver, or Woolly Bugger down to the fish will likely result in a strike as these fish don't see flies that often.

In the years since the opening of Blue Ridge, many of the surrounding lakes that also held bronzebacks were stocked with the Kentucky, or spotted, bass. Eventually, the "spots" out-competed the smallmouth and their range in Georgia was drastically reduced.

Unfortunately, spots have also found their way into this reservoir (The Georgia DNR recommends keeping a limit of spots whenever possible in order to help the smallmouth bass stick around). Fortunately, though, the smallies in Blue Ridge Reservoir are not only hanging around, but are actually doing quite well. Through the illegal stocking of bluebacks into the lake, the smallmouths have grown to some pretty hefty weights. Two- to three-pound fish are a common catch here and four- and five-pounders are a possibility. Just remember that if you land one of these beauties and they seem a little livid, don't take it personally.

Blue Ridge is home to some large smallmouth bass.

Types of Fish
The main attraction is the smallmouth bass but spotted, largemouth, and white bass, walleye, and yellow perch are also possibilities.

Known Hatches
The smallmouth bass, when seen busting the surface, are generally feeding on blueback herring. Mayflies are also seen regularly on the surface of the lake.

Equipment to Use
Rods: 6 to 8 weight rods, 9 to 10 feet in length
Reels: Standard disc drag
Lines: Floating weight-forward or double-taper to match rod weight
Leaders: 6- to 9-foot leaders tapered to 6- to 8-pound test
Wading: A boat is a necessity on this deep mountain lake.

Flies to Use
Surface Flies: #4-6 DP Popper, #4-6 DP Slider, #10 Deer Hair Popper, #6 Dahlberg Diver, #2-10 Gaines Sneaky Pete, #4-8 Blados's Crease Fly.

Sub-surface Flies: #1/0 Enrico's Shad, #4-10 Krystal Bugger, #4-10 Woolly Bugger, #4-6 Woolly Grubber, #4-10 Muddler Minnow, #4-8 White Beadhead Flash Zonker, #4-8 Zonker, #4-8 Conehead Double Bunny, #2/0-2 Clouser Minnow, #1 Cowen's Coyote, #1/0-2 Lefty's Deceiver, #2-8 Chocklett's Gummy Minnow.

When to Fish
Prime-time for catching surface-feeding smallmouth bass with a fly rod is in April, May, October, and November. However, there is a chance of seeing rising smallies or hooking subsurface smallies on the lake almost any day of the year.

Seasons & Limits
The lake is governed under general regulations except that up to 15 walleye may be kept per angler per day, as opposed to 8 in other Georgia fisheries. Please keep a limit of spotted bass (10) whenever possible to help sustain the smallmouth.

Nearby Fly Fishing
The Toccoa River tailwater coming out of the lake or the Toccoa River delayed harvest section upstream of the lake are both great places to fish. Feeder creeks of the upper river like Noontootla, Jones, and a host of other streams I dare not mention are accessible, as well. The pay-to-fish section of Noontootla Creek, Noontootla Creek Farms, is also just a short drive away.

Accommodations & Services
Hotels and restaurants abound in the town of Blue Ridge. In the downtown area, a fully stocked fly shop and guide service, Unicoi Outfitters, can help you get on fish. Guides Nathan Lewis, Bob Borgwat, and Kent Klewein guide fly anglers on this lake, as well.

Helpful Web Sites
UnicoiOutfitters.com, Kent-Klewein.com
ReelAnglingAdventures.com, TVA.com

Rating
When the smallmouth bite is on there is no match for this fishery in the entire state. And even when the smallies aren't hitting topwater consistently, there is almost always a chance for one. I give it an 8 out of 10.

*Jimmy Harris stays low and out of sight
in hopes of hooking a native brook trout.*

Brook Trout Streams

I knew while planning this book that casting flies for *Salvelinus fontinalis* would have to be included. And how could it not be? It's our only native salmonid and an important part of the fly fishing culture in the Peach State. But, because of the fact that almost all brookie streams in our state can handle only the lightest of fishing pressure and because I don't want to give away anyone's favorite speck stream—or have a bounty on my head—I've decided to present this chapter in as vague a manner as possible. Keep in mind that these fish have suffered a drastic decline in both numbers and range over the last century, so take as much care as possible to release them unharmed.

While I can't give away stream names, I can at least offer a few hints on finding brookie waters. The easiest way to search is to volunteer for a Trout Unlimited workday taking place on a brook trout stream. The Back-the-Brookie campaign is in full swing in our state and plenty of these projects are on the calendars. You will benefit by learning a few secret spots and the brook trout will benefit from your hard work.

Types of Fish
Well . . . Brook trout.

Known Hatches
Refer to the Southern Appalachian Freestone Streams Hatch Chart on page 17.

Equipment to Use
Rods: 0-3 weight, 5 to 7 feet in length.
Reels: Any reel that will hold your fly line!
Lines: Floating to match rod weight.
Leaders: 5X-7X leaders, 7½ to 9 feet in length.
Wading: Generally hip- or waist-high waders are sufficient for these tiny headwater streams. Another option is to wear a good pair of hiking boots and navigate the banks of the creeks.

Flies to Use
Dry Flies: #16-20 Elk Hair Caddis, #16-18 BWO, #16-22 Adams, #16-22 Adams Parachute, #16-20 Adams Irresistible, #18-22 Griffith's Gnat, #16-22 Light Cahill Dun, #16-22 Light Cahill Parachute, #14-18 Stimulator, #14-18 Royal Coachman, #14-18 Royal Wulff, #14-18 Royal Trude, #14-18 Yellow Humpy.

Nymphs & Wet Flies: #12-20 Prince Nymph, #12-20 Hare's Ear Nymph, #12-16 Zug Bug, #12-20 Pheasant Tail, #18-22 Midge Pupa, #16-20 Black Stonefly Nymph, #14-16 Yellow Stonefly Nymph, #4-8 Golden Stonefly Nymph, #4-8 Black Stonefly Nymph,

Continued

Jimmy Harris casts under a culvert on a top-secret brook trout stream.

Fishing for brook trout almost always involves casting in very tight quarters.

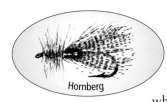
Hornberg

If you want to make it a bit more challenging for yourself, there is another way to go about it. The first step is to pick up a *Trout Streams of Georgia* map, which is available through the Georgia Department of Natural Resource's Wildlife Resource Division. After doing that, compare the seasonal streams on that map with a topographic map—most all of the streams that contain brook trout are seasonal, east of the town of Blue Ridge, and found at elevations of 2,200 feet and higher.

Pick a few streams that fit this criteria, plot out your driving directions while cross-referencing a map that lists Forest Service roads, pack your smallest fly rod and a handful of attractor dry flies and hit the road. Once you reach your destination, you'll likely need to find the barrier falls and fish above them to find the brook trout. Many of the streams in north Georgia were stocked with rainbows, browns, or both at some point and because they can outcompete brook trout, falls high enough to block passage of the dominant fishes almost always need to be present to sustain a population of brookies.

If you're lucky enough to actually find a brookie stream, only half the battle is over. Hacking through jungles of rhododendron and over steep terrain is tasking to say the least. And to think, all of this for a three-inch fish!

To help the brook trout, and to help yourself find brookie waters, lend a hand with Georgia's Back-the-Brookie campaign. Learn more at georgiatu.org.

Flies to Use (continued)
#18-22 Disco Midge, #18-22 Zebra Midge, #16-22 Soft Hackle Wet, #16-22 Soft Hackle Pheasant Tail Nymph, #18-20 Lightning Bug, #12-14 Hornberg, #12-14 Yellarhammer.

When to Fish
Exploring "blue lines" can be fun any time they are legal to fish, but steer clear of any redds visible during spawning season—this occurs in fall for the brook trout. Most anglers pursue brookies in the heat of the summer, when other lower-elevation creeks are too warm to fish, as these creeks remain nice and cool.

Seasons & Limits
There are some year-round brook trout streams in Georgia, but most are seasonal streams. While keeping eight trout is legal in our state, you would probably get more meat off of one stocked rainbow trout. Catch and release of these jewels is highly encouraged.

Helpful Information
georgiatu.org/html/back_the_brookie.html

Rating
The thrill of stalking our state's only native salmonid across rugged mountains, in this case a char that has survived here for millennia, warrants a 9 out of 10 for the overall experience.

The majority of native brook trout caught in Georgia waters are small, but well worth the effort.

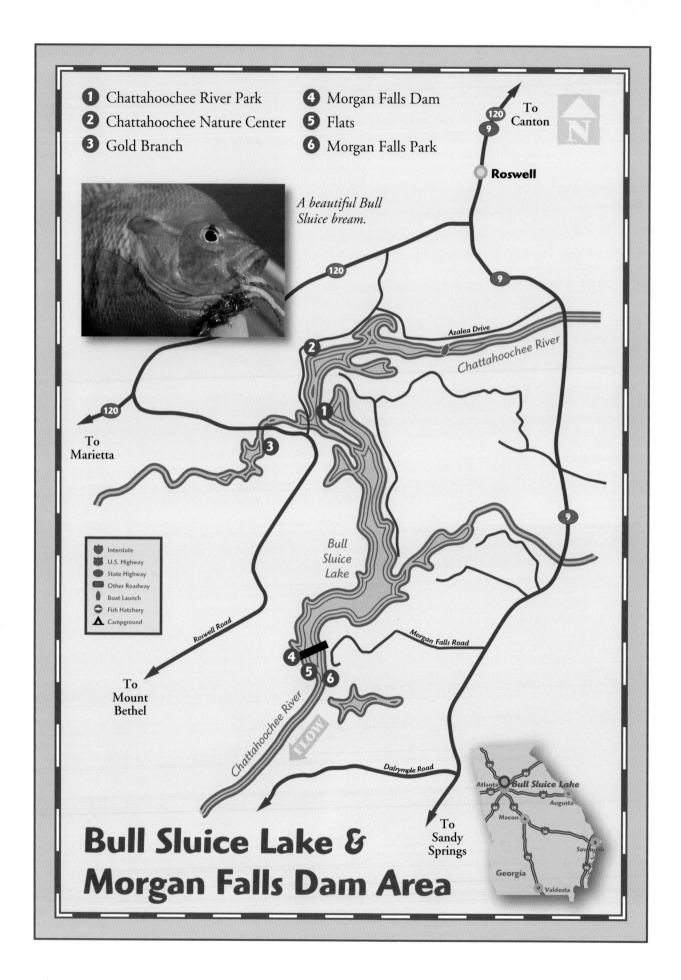

1. Chattahoochee River Park
2. Chattahoochee Nature Center
3. Gold Branch
4. Morgan Falls Dam
5. Flats
6. Morgan Falls Park

A beautiful Bull Sluice bream.

To Canton

Roswell

To Marietta

Azalea Drive

Chattahoochee River

To Mount Bethel

Bull Sluice Lake

Legend:
- Interstate
- U.S. Highway
- State Highway
- Other Roadway
- Boat Launch
- Fish Hatchery
- Campground

Roswell Road

Morgan Falls Road

Chattahoochee River

FLOW

Dalrymple Road

To Sandy Springs

Bull Sluice Lake & Morgan Falls Dam Area

Atlanta — Bull Sluice Lake
Augusta
Macon
Savannah
Georgia
Valdosta

Bull Sluice Lake

& Morgan Falls Dam Area

On a sturdy and quiet mud flat, a large tail breaks above water as the rest of the 13-pound fish below feeds, slurping retreating prey from the bottom and leaving a cloudy perimeter wherever he goes. Nearby, an angler freezes at the sight of the tail some 70 feet away. Enough fly line is stripped from the reel to reveal a different type of line, one that he hopes will be sopping wet in a moment—the backing. A long, delicate cast is made and the fly makes a gentle floop as it enters the water and slowly sinks into the path of the tailer. Finally, the angler thinks, a fish I didn't spook—a huge victory by itself.

As the fish makes its way, the angler worries that his heart, which is pounding like a bass drum, might actually be pumping hard enough to send vibrations down into his flats boots and across the 70 feet of ankle-deep water, alerting the fish to his presence. But as the fish nears the fly, his tail climbs higher above the water's surface and the barely-detectable tick of a fish tasting a fly transfers through leader, line, rod, and reel. And with a violent tug on the line, the fly is strip-set into soft mouth, a mouth in stark contrast

Good carp flies usually have beadheads or chain eyes and rubber legs.

Fishing for carp requires a lot of stealth and patience.

Carp fanatics Jeff Gillespie (left) and Mark Ellis stalk
the "golden ghost" just below Morgan Falls Dam.

Ellis's Hook-Up Nymph

to the very hard run that follows. In a flash, 80 yards of backing are exactly as the angler desired—wet.

The tailing fish in this story isn't the mighty redfish or exalted bonefish, but a fish that is often labeled as a trash fish in angling circles, the lowly carp. And the mud flat where this scenario regularly takes place for two Georgia fly anglers, Mark Ellis and Jeff Gillespie, can be found on Bull Sluice Lake, an impoundment on the Chattahoochee River only a few hundred yards from apartment buildings and restaurants in Atlanta.

For years, Mark and Jeff have stalked golden ghosts on this 500-acre lake and on a flat just the other side of Morgan Falls Dam. Largemouth and shoal bass, stripers, and even browns and rainbows will show up in this area, but for Mark and Jeff, there is no challenge like the carp. Not only can these fish grow in excess of 20 pounds, they also rival any fish that swims when it comes to wariness, making it a very testing target on fly tackle.

When carp spawn on these flats in the spring—in late April and early May—they stack up by the thousands, many with their backs out of the water as they search for a mate and a spot to keep the circle of life, well, circulating. This time of year is the best time to get out and walk the flats or rig up a boat like Mark and Jeff have—a canoe with pontoons rigged to the side for stability and a poling platform on the back for stealthy hunting.

Despite several articles in regional and national fishing publications, these two say they have yet to see another fly flinger stalking these fish. So if you're up to the challenge and can peel yourself away from smaller and less-challenging species, test your skills on the cagey carp. And say hello to Mark and Jeff if you see them.

Angler Mark Ellis displays a fine Bull Sluice carp.
Photo by Jeff Gillespie.

Types of Fish

Carp, catfish, largemouth, shoal, and striped bass (below Morgan Falls Dam), bream, rainbow and brown trout.

Known Hatches

Carp will eat practically anything available including baitfish and leeches. The primary forage the carp enjoy is large (three- to five-inch) crawfish. However, carp will feed like trout on nymphs and have even been known to rise to hatching aquatic insects from time to time, so follow the Chattahoochee River Tailwater Hatch Chart and have the appropriate flies on hand, just in case.

Equipment to Use

Rods: 6 to 8 weight rods, 9 to 10 feet in length.
Reels: Standard disc drag
Lines: Floating weight-forward or double-taper to match rod weight.
Leaders: 9- to 15-foot leaders tapered to 2X to 4X tippet (fluorocarbon is preferred).
Wading: A boat with a shallow draft is a big help here, but wading these shallow flats is also a lot of fun. Wet-wade in the warmer months and go with chest waders during the cooler parts of the year.

Flies to Use

Carp Flies: Ellis's Bling-Cray, Ellis's Hook-Up Nymph, Crazy Charlie, Cowen's Bonefish Scampi, Whitlock's Crawfish.

Nymphs/Streamers: Woolly Bugger, Stonefly Nymph, Prince Nymph, Pheasant Tail Nymph, Hare's Ear Nymph.

When to Fish

Pre- and post-spawn, and during the spawn, too. Jeff Gillespie says that the fish here spawn, "April 12th, give or take" (somebody fishes here a lot). Carp can be targeted here year-round, though, particularly when water temps are above 55 degrees Fahrenheit. Still mornings with good light also allow anglers to sight-cast to feeding fish.

Seasons & Limits

For whatever reason, carp are not technically a game fish (maybe it's because they are too large or too difficult to catch), so there is no limit on them. Catch and release is encouraged, though.

Nearby Fly Fishing

The entire Chattahoochee Tailwater, including the delayed harvest section, flows into and out of this lake.

Accommodations & Services

Chris Scalley and his River Through Atlanta Guide Service can show you around the river as well as anyone. And, two local fly shops can set you up with the proper gear and flies, Fly Box Outfitters in Kennesaw and The Fish Hawk in Buckhead.

Helpful Information

Morgan Falls Dam Water Releases, (404) 329-1455

Rating

Big, challenging carp that are as spooky as any bonefish, tailing on flats just like a bonefish and taking backing as fast as bonefish, except right here in Atlanta means an easy 8 out of 10.

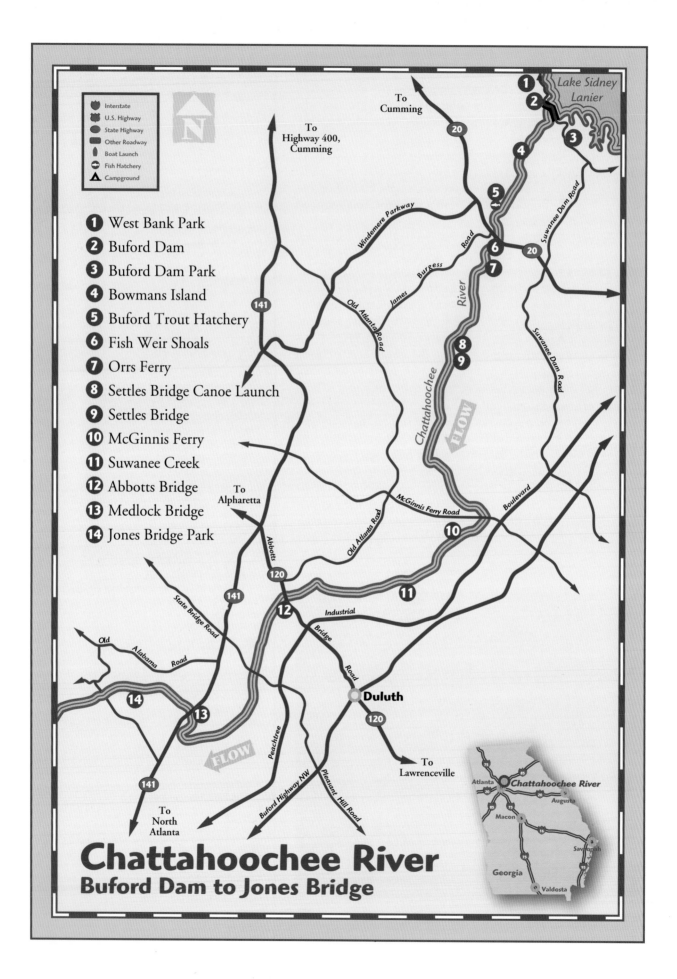

Legend:
- Interstate
- U.S. Highway
- State Highway
- Other Roadway
- Boat Launch
- Fish Hatchery
- Campground

1. West Bank Park
2. Buford Dam
3. Buford Dam Park
4. Bowmans Island
5. Buford Trout Hatchery
6. Fish Weir Shoals
7. Orrs Ferry
8. Settles Bridge Canoe Launch
9. Settles Bridge
10. McGinnis Ferry
11. Suwanee Creek
12. Abbotts Bridge
13. Medlock Bridge
14. Jones Bridge Park

Lake Sidney Lanier

To Cumming

To Highway 400, Cumming

Windemere Parkway

Burgess Road

Old Atlanta Road

James

Chattahoochee River

Suwanee Dam Road

FLOW

To Alpharetta

Old Atlanta Road

McGinnis Ferry Road

Boulevard

Abbotts

State Bridge Road

Industrial

Bridge

Road

Old Alabama Road

FLOW

Peachtree

Buford Highway NW

Pleasant Hill Road

Duluth

To Lawrenceville

To North Atlanta

Chattahoochee River
Buford Dam to Jones Bridge

Atlanta · Chattahoochee River
Augusta
Macon
Savannah
Georgia
Valdosta

Chattahoochee River

Buford Dam to Jones Bridge

When the mighty Chattahoochee River flows from the depths of Lake Sidney Lanier and out of Buford Dam, it appears as a changed river. Before the construction of the lake, the river in this section used to be a warmwater paradise, filled with bream and largemouth and shoal bass. After the construction of the dam the ensuing coldwaters forced those fish downstream and left an obvious void. Luckily for all of us, trout were placed in this new environment several years after the dam was built and have done well ever since.

As part of one of the great rivers of the South, the section from Buford Dam to Jones Bridge holds thousands of stocked rainbow trout thanks to the Buford Trout Hatchery that lies just downstream from the dam. Despite its Deep South geography, the river is also home to an abundance of wild brown trout, much to the surprise of many Atlantans who stereotype the river by saying things like, "I wouldn't touch that nasty water with a ten-foot pole." A good response to this is telling them that a nine-foot five-weight pole will suffice.

The fishing may draw you here, but it's safety on the river that should be top priority. Several people drown here every year

Continued

Kyle Burrell nymphing for trout near Abbotts Bridge. Photo by David Cannon.

Kyle Burrell works a deep run for wild Chattahoochee brown trout. Photo by David Cannon.

Chattahoochee River Tailwater Hatch Chart

Courtesy of Chris Scalley and the Chattahoochee Coldwater Fishery Foundation

Insect	Jan	Feb	Mar	April	May	June	July	Aug	Sept	Oct	Nov	Dec
Caddis												
Blue-Winged Olive												
Sulphur												
Yellow Drake												
Stonefly												
Midges												
Cranefly												
Scud												
Sowbug												
Terrestrials												
Crayfish												
Shad & Herring												
Sculpin												

Insect	Sizes	Dry Flies	Nymphs/Streamers
Caddis	14–20	X-Caddis, Elk Hair Caddis, Adams, Royal Wulff, Scalley's Cripple Caddis	LaFontaine Pupa, Hare's Ear Nymph, Prince Nymph, Z-Wing Caddis
Blue-Winged Olive	14–24	Adams, Parachute Adams, Compara Dun, Sparkle Dun	Pheasant Tail Nymph, Hare's Ear Nymph, Zug Bug, Barr's Emerger
Sulphur	18–20	Compara Dun, Sparkle Dun, Parachute Adams	Pheasant Tail Nymph, Hare's Ear Nymph, Barr's Emerger
Yellow Drake	12	Parachute Adams, Compara Dun, Schroeder's Hopper	Anytime-Anywhere, Pheasant Tail Nymph
Stonefly	4–16	Stimulator, Royal Trude, Elk Hair Caddis	Kaufmann's Stone, Anytime-Anywhere
Midges	16–24	Griffith's Gnat, Fitzsimmon's Midge, Adams, Bett's Emerger	Brassie, Serendipity
Cranefly	6–16	Schroeder's Hopper, Jack Dennis Cranefly, Scalley's Cranefly	Anytime-Anywhere, Peacock Simulator, Hare's Ear Nymph, Pheasant Tail Nymph
Scud	14–18	None	Hare's Ear Nymph, Kaufmann's Scud, Epoxy Scud
Sowbug	14–18	None	Hare's Ear Nymph, Kaufmann's Scud, Epoxy Scud
Terrestrials	6–24	Para-Ant, Foam Beetle, Dave's Hopper, Royal Wulff	Hardbody Ant, Woolly Worm, Pfitzer Special
Crayfish	6–12	None	Woolly Bugger, Borger Crayfish, Beadhead Leech
Shad & Herring	8–12	None	Clouser Minnow, Woolly Bugger, Pearl Zonker, Brer Rabbit
Sculpin	8–12	None	Whitlock's Sculpin, Woolhead Sculpin

Rooks's Berry Nymph

for lack of knowing how powerful the water releases are and when they are going to occur. To keep from becoming a statistic, Chattahoochee legend Don Pfitzer recommends putting a $20 bill on top of a rock while you're fishing. When you see the water from a release start to creep up that rock, it's time to snatch your money and get out of the water to live, and fish, another day.

As to fishing this section, if you are accustomed to freestone rivers, don't make the mistake of assuming that a tailwater like the Chattahoochee fishes the same way. While freestone rivers go through periods of drought and flood, a tailwater experiences both every day. Because of its close proximity to the dam and the scourging effects of the powerful flows, less vegetation clings to the river bottom in this section compared to the river farther downstream, which results in less bug life here than in stretches farther downriver.

The spring months here are characterized by abundances of bug life. Virtually every invertebrate, from mayflies to scuds, sees an explosion of life during this time of year. It's thought that a trout can put on as much as one third of its yearly growth weight over this time period, making it a good time for a trout angler to be presenting flies to these gorgers.

In mid-May, terrestrial food sources such as ants, Japanese beetles hanging on muscadine vines, grasshoppers from surrounding fields and lawns, and Catawba worms clinging to the leaves of Catawba trees become the main food sources for the trout. Combined with crustaceans like scuds and sowbugs, these groceries keep the fish fat and happy through summer and fall.

In late fall, Lake Sidney Lanier experiences the phenomenon known as lake turnover and the Chattahoochee above Jones Bridge turns a pea-green color and stays that way for several weeks. But, like the rest of the year on this great river, fish can still be caught with regularity.

The wild brown trout in the Chattahoochee can display some remarkable colors. Photo by David Cannon.

Flies to Use (continued)

Hopper, #4-16 Stimulator, #4-16 Royal Trude, #16-24 Griffith's Gnat, #16-24 Fitzsimmon's Midge, #16-24 Bett's Emerger, #6-16 Jack Dennis Cranefly, #6-16 Scalley's Daddy Long-leg, #6-24 Para Ant, #6-12 Foam Beetle, #6-14 Dave's Hopper, #12-14 Blue Humpy.

Nymphs: #14-20 LaFontaine Pupa, #6-20 Hare's Ear Nymph, #14-24, Prince Nymph, #14-20 Z-Wing Caddis, #6-24 Scalley's CDC Pheasant Tail Nymph, #14-24 Zug Bug, #14-24 Barr's Emerger, #4-16 Anytime-Anywhere, #4-16 Kaufmann's Stone, #16-24 Brassie, #16-24 Serendipity, #6-16 Peacock Simulator, #14-18 Kaufmann's Scud, #14-18 Epoxy Scud, #12-20 Hardbody Ant, #6-14 Woolly Worm, #10-14 Pfitzer Special, #6-12 Borger Crayfish, #14 Kyle's Copperhead, #16-18 Kyle's 'Hoochee Caddis, #16-20 Blue Assassin, #14-18 Rooks's Berry Nymph, #16-20 Lightning Bug, #16-20 Rainbow Warrior, #14-18 Scalley's Miracle Nymph, #14 San Juan Worm, #14 Y2K Bug, #10 Hurless Nymph.

Streamers: #6-10 Krystal Bugger, #6-10 Woolly Bugger, #6-10 Muddler Minnow, #8 White Beadhead Flash Zonker, #8 Zonker, #6-10 Mickey Finn, #6-10 Black-nosed Dace, #8-12 Scalley's Bugsy-Shad, #6-12 Scalley's Electric Bugger, #8-12 Clouser Minnow, #8-12 Brer Rabbit, #8-12 Whitlock's Sculpin, #8-12 Woolhead Sculpin.

When to Fish

Consistently cold water coming from the depths of Lake Sidney Lanier make this portion of the river very good 12 months of the year.

Seasons & Limits

From Buford Dam to the Georgia Highway 20 Bridge, a floatation device must be worn by anyone on the river at all times. Also, only artificial lures may be used in the section from 20 Bridge downstream to the boat ramp at Medlock Bridge (just upstream of Georgia Highway 141). From the dam down to Peachtree Creek and within the Chattahoochee River National Recreation Area, the river cannot be used from 30 minutes after sunset to 30 minutes before sunrise. Visit GoFishGeorgia.com for details.

Nearby Fly Fishing

On the other side of Buford Dam, Lake Sidney Lanier holds some big stripers and spotted bass, both of which will take flies. Or, head downstream to fish the Jones Bridge to Morgan Falls Dam section.

Accommodations & Services

Several fly shops service this area including The Orvis Store in Buckhead and the White River Fly Shop inside of Bass Pro Shops in Lawrenceville. The River Through Atlanta Guide Service also guides anglers here.

Helpful Information

RiverThroughAtlanta.com
Orvis.com
BassPro.com
nps.gov/chat

Buford Dam Water Release Schedule: water.sam.usace.army.mil. Or call (770) 945-1466.

Rating

Plenty of stocked rainbows and wild brown trout with great accessibility and a sense of being farther away from a huge city than you actually are makes this a 9 out of 10.

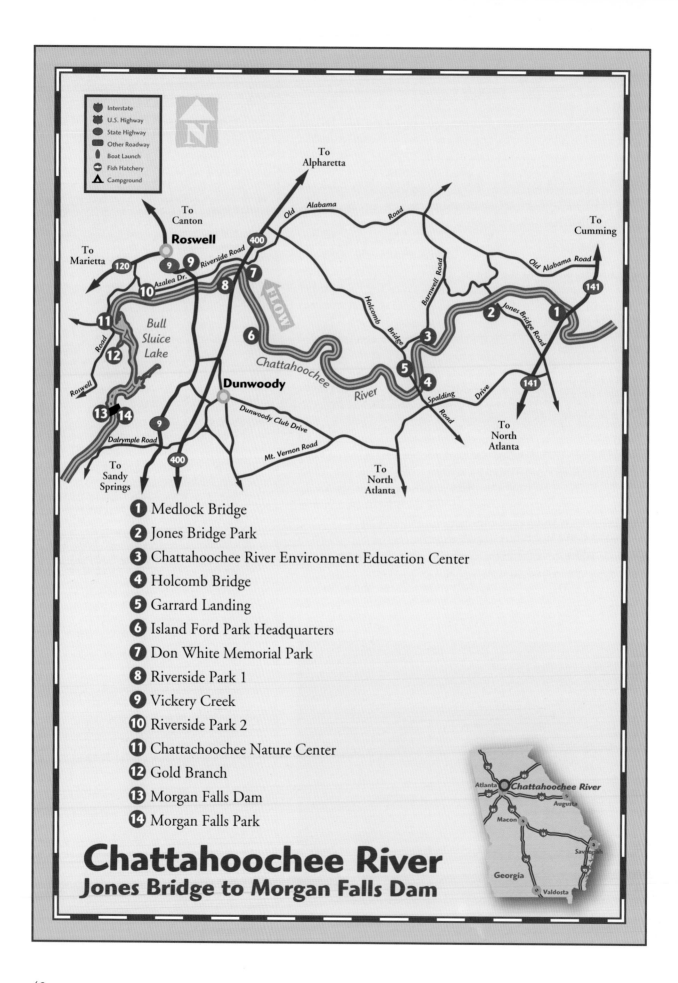

Legend:
- Interstate
- U.S. Highway
- State Highway
- Other Roadway
- Boat Launch
- Fish Hatchery
- Campground

1. Medlock Bridge
2. Jones Bridge Park
3. Chattahoochee River Environment Education Center
4. Holcomb Bridge
5. Garrard Landing
6. Island Ford Park Headquarters
7. Don White Memorial Park
8. Riverside Park 1
9. Vickery Creek
10. Riverside Park 2
11. Chattachoochee Nature Center
12. Gold Branch
13. Morgan Falls Dam
14. Morgan Falls Park

Chattahoochee River
Jones Bridge to Morgan Falls Dam

Chattahoochee River

Jones Bridge to Morgan Falls Dam

The year is 1960. It's a dark and nervous night. Three men, all die-hard outdoorsmen and lay-wildlife biologists, quietly wait on the edge of the Chattahoochee River, somewhere not far downstream from Jones Bridge. Yes, the men are technically "legal" as they've obtained permission from a landowner to be here and perform the task at hand. But they'd rather not draw any unwanted attention to themselves. As their hearts pound with the excitement that comes with the possibility of getting caught, a set of headlights appears in the distance.

As the beams grow brighter and nearer, the faint sound of Ray Charles belting one of the biggest hits of the year, "Georgia On My Mind," is barely audible beneath the frothing of aerating water. Ironically, Georgia is on all of their minds, and more specifically, Georgia law enforcement.

The driver sets the brake and chocks a rear tire. His knees are stiff from the long ride from North Carolina. As buckets are handed

Types of Fish
Rainbow and brown trout.

Known Hatches
Caddis, Blue-Winged Olives, Sulphur Mayflies, Yellow Drake Mayflies, Big Golden Stoneflies, Winter Black Stoneflies, Midges, Terrestrials, Craneflies. Forage also includes Scuds, Sowbugs, Crayfish, and Sculpin. Also, if a shad kill occurs during a cold winter, water releases from the dam can send dead shad this far down the river.

Equipment to Use
Rods: 4-5 weights for nymphs and dry flies, 6-7 weights for streamers. Both should be 8½ to 10 feet long.
Reels: Larger fish do reside here, so a reel with a disc drag is appropriate.
Lines: Floating lines to match rod weight when fishing dries or nymphs, intermediate lines to match rod weight when fishing streamers.
Leaders: 9- to 12-foot leaders in either 3X or 4X when fishing floating lines, 5- to 7-foot leaders tapered from 1-3X when fishing intermediate lines.
Wading: Floating in a drift boat, Jon boat, belly boat or pontoon is the best way to see the 'Hooch. However, shoals at certain access points are great for wading while wearing chest waders.

Flies to Use
See the Chattahoochee River Tailwater Hatch Chart to correctly match the hatch.

Continued

Anglers fishing the Chattahoochee at midday.
Photo by David Cannon.

Zach Middlebrooks displaying an amazing 'Hooch brown trout. Photo by Chris Scalley.

Conehead Woolly Bugger

out, the cover of darkness is briefly surrendered for the sake of lighting a path with Coleman lanterns hooked to branches overhanging the river. "10,000 fingerling rainbow trout?" the driver asks. "Yes sir," replies the ringleader of the Chattahoochee's very first bucket brigade. "The boss threw in 2,000 browns at no charge to say thanks for your patronage," said the driver. And for the next couple of hours, dip nets and strong backs work with the aid of an ample dose of adrenaline.

And with that, one of the finest trout fisheries in the Southeast was born. Over the coming decades, the river would evolve into something that its first "volunteers" could have only hoped—viable waters for the state to manage both with stocked- and self-sustaining populations of browns and rainbows.

The part of the Chattahoochee flowing from the ruins of the old Jones Bridge down to Morgan Falls Dam, according to long-time guide and river expert Chris Scalley, is a trout stream worthy of blue ribbon status. While it still benefits from the cold releases of water from the bottom of Lake Sidney Lanier, the not-so-positive effects of the releases such as scourging of vegetation and discoloration from lake turnover aren't felt quite as much. With plenty of aquatic vegetation, prolific bug life, and clear water, this section could be described as a spring creek with a hydroelectric dam as its source.

Going after the trout along this run is a bit different from chasing them upstream of Jones Bridge or below Morgan Falls Dam. The abundance of food and the presence of plenty of wild browns can make for some challenging fishing at times. On the other hand, presenting a fly that is a close imitation of what the trout are keyed in on at the right time can yield the catching of great numbers of fat, healthy fish.

To keep it simple, work the obvious fish lies in the river. Seams of water between fast currents and slack water, woody debris lining the banks and holding thousands of cased caddis, gravel bars, and vegetated areas will all attract and hold trout. If you spot a weed bed in the river, cast your fly to it and work the area thoroughly. Aquatic insects will be clinging to the vegetation, and where there are aquatic insects, the trout won't be far behind. And when that trout latches onto your fly, be thankful for the bravery of three men who risked their good names for the sake of fishing.

A nice fall brown that fell to a Scalley's Electric Bugger stripped upstream. Photo by David Cannon.

Flies to Use (continued)

Dry Flies: #14-20 X-Caddis, #4-20 Elk Hair Caddis, #12-24 Adams, #12-24 Adams Parachute, #6-24 Royal Wulff, #14-20 Scalley's Crippled Caddis, #14-24 Comparadun, #14-24 Sparkle Dun, #6-16 Schroeder's Hopper, #4-16 Stimulator, #4-16 Royal Trude, #16-24 Griffith's Gnat, #16-24 Fitzsimmon's Midge, #16-24 Bett's Emerger, #6-16 Jack Dennis Cranefly, #6-16 Scalley's Daddy Long-leg, #6-24 Para Ant, #6-12 Foam Beetle, #6-14 Dave's Hopper, #12-14 Blue Humpy.

Nymphs: #14-20 LaFontaine Pupa, #6-20 Hare's Ear Nymph, #14-24, Prince Nymph, #14-20 Z-Wing Caddis, #6-24 Scalley's CDC Pheasant Tail Nymph, #14-24 Zug Bug, #14-24 Barr's Emerger, #4-16 Anytime-Anywhere, #4-16 Kaufmann's Stone, #16-24 Brassie, #16-24 Serendipity, #6-16 Peacock Simulator, #14-18 Kaufmann's Scud, #14-18 Epoxy Scud, #12-20 Hardbody Ant, #6-14 Woolly Worm, #10-14 Pfitzer Special, #6-12 Borger Crayfish, #14 Kyle's Copperhead, #16-18 Kyle's 'Hoochee Caddis, #16-20 Blue Assassin, #14-18 Rooks's Berry Nymph, #16-20 Lightning Bug, #16-20 Rainbow Warrior, #14-18 Scalley's Miracle Nymph, #14 San Juan Worm, #14 Y2K Bug, #10 Hurless Nymph.

Streamers: #6-10 Krystal Bugger, #6-10 Woolly Bugger, #6-10 Muddler Minnow, #8 White Beadhead Flash Zonker, #8 Zonker, #6-10 Mickey Finn, #6-10 Black-nosed Dace, #8-12 Scalley's Bugsy-Shad, #6-12 Scalley's Electric Bugger, #8-12 Clouser Minnow, #8-12 Brer Rabbit, #8-12 Whitlock's Sculpin, #8-12 Woolhead Sculpin.

When to Fish
This is great water from January through December.

Seasons & Limits
This run can be fished all year and falls under general regulations. Visit GoFishGeorgia.com for complete regulations.

Nearby Fly Fishing
On the other side of Buford Dam, Lake Sidney Lanier holds some big stripers and spotted bass, both of which will take flies. Or, head upstream to fish the Buford Dam to Jones Bridge section.

Accommodations & Services
Several fly shops service this area including The Orvis Store in Norcross, the White River Fly Shop inside of Bass Pro Shops in Lawrenceville, The Fish Hawk and The Orvis Store in Buckhead and Fly Box Outfitters in Kennesaw. The River Through Atlanta Guide Service operates on this stretch.

Helpful Information
RiverThroughAtlanta.com
Orvis.com
BassPro.com
nps.gov/chat

Buford Dam Water Release Schedule:
water.sam.usace.army.mil
Or call (770) 945-1466.

Rating
It's a tailwater with the qualities of a spring creek. That sounds like a 10 to me.

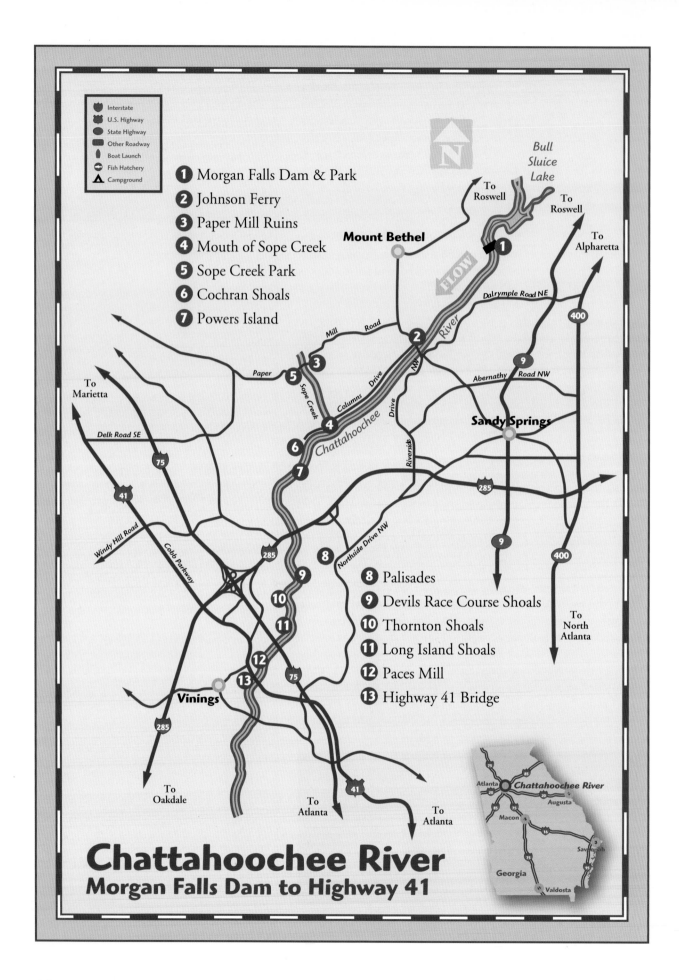

Interstate
U.S. Highway
State Highway
Other Roadway
Boat Launch
Fish Hatchery
Campground

1. Morgan Falls Dam & Park
2. Johnson Ferry
3. Paper Mill Ruins
4. Mouth of Sope Creek
5. Sope Creek Park
6. Cochran Shoals
7. Powers Island

8. Palisades
9. Devils Race Course Shoals
10. Thornton Shoals
11. Long Island Shoals
12. Paces Mill
13. Highway 41 Bridge

To Roswell
To Roswell
To Alpharetta
Bull Sluice Lake
Mount Bethel
FLOW
Dalrymple Road NE
400
9
Abernathy Road NW
Sandy Springs
Mill Road
Paper
Sope Creek
Columns Drive
Chattahoochee
Drive
Riverside
River
NW
To Marietta
Delk Road SE
75
41
Windy Hill Road
Cobb Parkway
285
285
9
Northside Drive NW
400
To North Atlanta
9
10
11
12
13
75
Vinings
285
To Oakdale
To Atlanta
41
To Atlanta

Chattahoochee River
Morgan Falls Dam to Highway 41

Atlanta
Chattahoochee River
Augusta
Macon
Georgia
Savannah
Valdosta

Chattahoochee River

Morgan Falls Dam to Highway 41

In case the first 35 miles of fantastic water upstream wasn't enough, the all-too-generous Chattahoochee River just keeps on giving. The portion of the 'Hooch tailwater flowing out of Bull Sluice Lake via Morgan Falls Dam and down to the Highway 41 Bridge offers the angler more trout, some fine shoal bass fishing and even the shot at a hefty striped bass. Anyone who tells you that fishing in Georgia is no good needs to spend a few days here.

While there are some holdover trout on this stretch from year to year, the majority of what you'll be catching will be stocked browns and rainbows. Unlike the run from Buford Dam to Morgan Falls Dam, the water here isn't as kind to trout attempting to reproduce. So, the wild, reproducing browns and rainbows that are commonly seen upstream just can't do their thing in this warmer water. However, the water is perfectly suited for trout from about October through May, and sometimes longer in cooler, wetter years. This is one of the reasons why one of our five stream sections governed under delayed harvest regulations lies here.

What's really been gaining in popularity in recent years is the gathering of anglers to drift down the river in flotillas in search of shoal and smallmouth bass. We'll discuss this fish in more detail in the Flint River chapter, as it is one of the only other rivers in

On this section of the 'Hooch, trout, shoal bass, and even smallmouth bass can be expected on nearly any cast.

Duane Stalnaker fishes one of his favorite sections on the Chattahoochee.

Elk Hair Caddis

the state—and in the world—that houses this spectacular game fish.

Going after shoalies is as easy as rigging up your seven- or eight-weight fly rod with some floating line, a 2X leader, a fly of your choice, and covering the shoal areas. Good flies to throw for these fish are Clouser Minnows, Cowen's Coyotes, white Woolly Buggers, or Dahlberg Divers. Work your fly in shoal areas on the river. Just about any shoal bass caught on this section of the river could easily be played and landed on a lighter rod. But, a seven- or eight-weight will aid in casting bushier flies and come in handy in case you should happen upon one of the other larger inhabitants of the river.

Whether it's the cooler water, the abundance of stocked trout or perhaps both, stripers show up in decent numbers throughout this stretch in the summer. Stripers are regularly spotted under the 41 Bridge and all the way up to the outflow of Morgan Falls Dam. Targeting them, however, can be difficult. Low-light conditions, such as early morning, late evening or a cloudy day, are the best times to target these fish. Of course, one may decide to grab your Woolly Bugger as you're dead-drifting it for trout. Angler Jamie Sullivan, who was testing a new five-weight fly rod on some shoal bass, experienced this exact scenario. An eight-pound striper took his fly, which was tied to 1X tippet, and fought for almost an entire hour before Jamie was able to land it. You don't have to believe it if you don't want to. Spend some time on this section and find out for yourself.

Shoal and smallmouth bass alike inhabit this stretch of the river and are glad to grab hold of a Clouser Minnow.

Flies to Use (continued)

Shoal Bass & Striper Flies:

Surface Flies: #2-6 Kent's Stealth Bomber, #4-6 DP Popper, #4-6 DP Slider, #4-8 Sneaky Pete, #1/0-2 Blados's Crease Fly, #2-4 Pencil Popper.

Subsurface Flies: #2-8 Woolly Bugger, #10 Carter's Rubber-legged Dragon, #1/0-2 Clouser Minnow, #2-8 Muddler Minnow, #1 Cowen's Coyote.

When to Fish

This section is good for trout from October through May, but warm summer temperatures put the kibosh on summertime. However, shoal bass and stripers are present here in good numbers when the water warms, so there's no need to stop fishing this area for any period throughout the year.

Seasons & Limits

The section from the mouth of Sope Creek down to the Highway 41 Bridge falls under delayed harvest regulations from November 1 through May 14 of each year. All other areas fall under general fishing regulations. Visit GoFishGeorgia.com for complete regulations.

Nearby Fly Fishing

Bull Sluice Lake just upstream of Morgan Falls Dam is an awesome place to try to catch a carp on the fly rod. Other than that, the rest of the Chattahoochee tailwater upstream of Morgan Falls is wonderful year-round.

Accommodations & Services

The River Through Atlanta Guide Service team runs trips in this area and can help an angler target any of the species present here. This part of the river flows through north Atlanta, so dining and lodging opportunities abound. The Orvis Store in Norcross, The Orvis Store and The Fish Hawk in Buckhead, or Fly Box Outfitters in Kennesaw can outfit an angler for any species.

Helpful Information

RiverThroughAtlanta.com
Orvis.com
TheFishHawk.com
FlyBoxOutfitters.com
ChattahoocheeFoodWebs.org (hatch chart)
GeorgiaRiverFishing.com
nps.gov/chat
Morgan Falls Dam Water Release Schedule,
(404) 329-1455

Rating

This section of the Chattahoochee offers plenty of diversity, from catch and release trout to aggressive shoal bass to big striped bass and now even smallmouth bass. It deserves nothing less than an 9 out of 10.

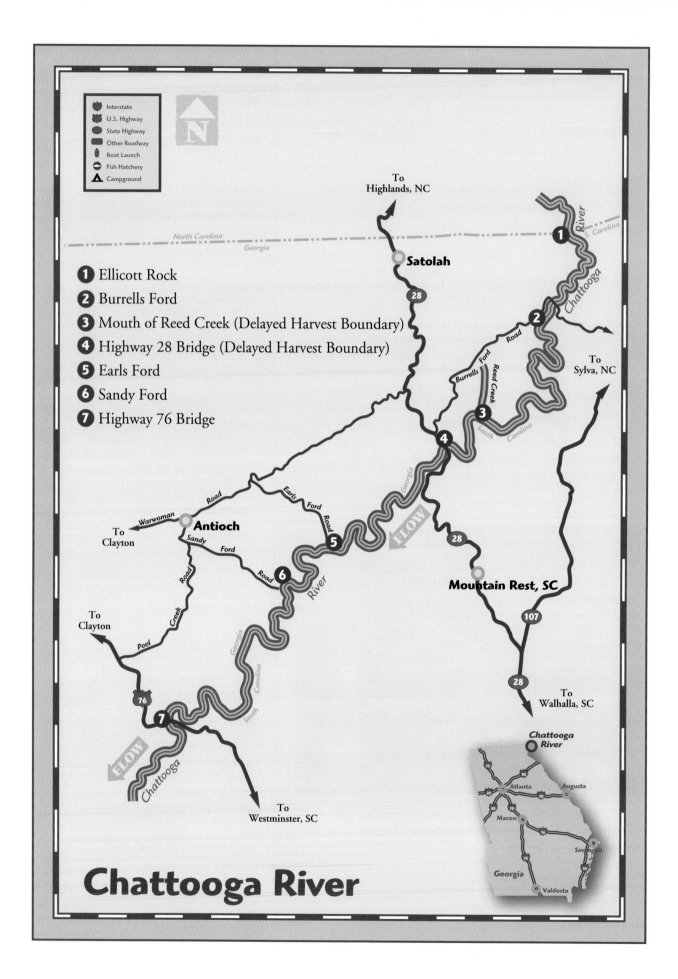

Legend:
- Interstate
- U.S. Highway
- State Highway
- Other Roadway
- Boat Launch
- Fish Hatchery
- Campground

1 Ellicott Rock
2 Burrells Ford
3 Mouth of Reed Creek (Delayed Harvest Boundary)
4 Highway 28 Bridge (Delayed Harvest Boundary)
5 Earls Ford
6 Sandy Ford
7 Highway 76 Bridge

To Highlands, NC

Satolah

North Carolina
Georgia

S. Carolina

Chattooga River

Burrells Ford Road

Reed Creek

To Sylva, NC

South Carolina

Georgia

To Clayton

Warwoman Road

Antioch

Earls Ford Road

Sandy Ford Road

28

Mountain Rest, SC

River

107

To Clayton

Pool Creek Road

Georgia
South Carolina

76

28

To Walhalla, SC

FLOW

Chattooga

To Westminster, SC

Chattooga River

Chattooga River

Atlanta
Augusta
Macon
Savannah
Georgia
Valdosta

Chattooga River

Chattooga River

The most torturous part of the fly fishing experience, for me at least, is the few minutes spent in the parking lot pulling on waders and cramming thick-socked feet into boots that seem to take hours to tie. In one of the few parking lots alongside the stretch of the Chattooga River from Ellicott Rock to the Highway 76 Bridge, this process seems even more agonizing.

But after only a few hundred paces, when the river comes into view, the worries of life, the thoughts of responsibility, and even the misery of parking lot prep dissolve in the almost magical waters now within reach. Each physical stride deeper into the Chattooga backcountry turns into a gait of miles for the soul as an awareness that a desk and a computer, a cell phone and a TV are far more foreign surroundings for you and your kind than is this place.

Arriving here at a favorite fishing hole—where mayflies and caddisflies flutter in the spring, changing leaves contrast against evergreens in the fall, or cold keeps crowds indoors in the winter—is like returning home. That home might lie somewhere near Ellicott Rock where the Chattooga leaves North Carolina to form the Georgia-South Carolina border. Or maybe it's near Burrells Ford, the Highway 28 Bridge, or the Highway 76 Bridge. Or perhaps it's a spot somewhere in between that dare not be discussed in print or even amongst good friends!

Wherever it is, the Chattooga is unique in that it's one of the only rivers in the eastern U.S. that doesn't have a road paralleling it, the result of the native Cherokees who used to inhabit this land viewing the river as a sacred place, one that they would only cross in a few places. Some say Chattooga is translated from the Cherokee word *Tsatu-gi*, which is thought to mean "has crossed the stream."

When the river first crosses into Georgia, it is creek-sized and is home to wild browns that are infamous for being spooky,

Types of Fish

Stocked brook trout, wild and stocked brown trout, wild and stocked rainbow trout, redeye bass, and bream are the most frequent Chattooga catches.

Known Hatches

Small Dun Caddis, Blue-Winged Olive, Blue Quill Mayfly, Midges, Winter Black Stonefly, Quill Gordon Mayfly, Light Cahill Mayfly, Early Black Stonefly, Cream Caddis, Red Quill/Hendrickson, March Brown Mayfly, Yellow Stonefly, Golden Stonefly, Speckled Grey Caddis, Giant Black Stonefly, Sulphur Mayfly, Green Drake Mayfly, Coffin Fly (Green Drake Spinner).

Equipment to Use

Rods: 4-6 weight, 8 to 10 feet in length.
Reels: Standard disc drag.
Lines: Floating weight-forward or double-taper to match rod weight.
Leaders: For trout, 4X-6X leaders, 9 to 15 feet in length; For redeye bass, 2X-4X leaders, 5 to 7 feet in length.
Wading: Chest waders will allow you to navigate some of the deeper areas of the Chattooga, but May through September are wet-wading friendly.

Flies to Use

See the Southern Appalachian Freestone Hatch Chart to correctly match the hatch.

Dry Flies: #8-20 Adams, #8-20 Adams Parachute, #16-20 Blue Quill #16-20 BWO, #16-22 Griffith's Gnat, #16-20 Black Elk Hair Caddis, #18 Brown Elk Hair Caddis, #12-14 Quill Gordon, #14-16 Red Quill, #14-16 Hendrickson, #8-14 March Brown, #8-14 March Brown Parachute, #14-16 Yellow Stimulator, #14-16 Yellow Elk Hair Caddis, #12-18 Light Cahill, #12-18 Light Cahill Parachute, #14-18 Sulphur Comparadun, #14-18 Cream Variant, #8-14 Blue Dun Parachute, #8-10 Green Drake, #8-10 Spent-wing Coffin Fly, #8-10 Parachute Coffin Fly, #8-10 Light Cahill Parachute, #14-16 Dark Elk Hair Caddis with Green, #14-16 Dark Elk Hair Caddis with Yellow and Brown, #20-22 Parachute Trico, #20-22 Black Poly Wing Spinner #8-10 Ginger Elk Hair Caddis.

Continued

A Chattooga River rainbow is landed and will soon be released.

The Chattooga offers unparalleled scenery and good fishing, too.

Light Cahill

nocturnal and, for someone new to the river, possibly non-existent.

The next downstream access point, Burrells Ford, is heavily stocked with browns and rainbows . . . and campers. A short hike in either direction of the bridge—particularly downstream, where more stocked fish wash down—will put some distance between you and the camper/angler (not to be confused with the angler/camper).

The area between Burrells Ford and the next downstream access, the Highway 28 Bridge, is stocked via helicopter with fingerling trout, a collaborative effort of the Rabun and Saluda chapters of Trout Unlimited, the U.S. Forest Service, and both Georgia's and South Carolina's DNR. These fish grow up wild and can be as tough as the wild browns upstream.

The area from the mouth of Reed Creek downstream to the 28 Bridge falls under delayed harvest regulations (see page 135 for details) and is more beginner-friendly. Though it's too warm for trout from June through September, this area and downstream to the 76 Bridge are prime for the native redeye bass.

Whatever spot on the Chattooga becomes home to you, please respect the safety concerns that come along with traveling the backcountry and the qualities that made this Congress's first choice for the Wild and Scenic Rivers designation back in 1974. And if someone should ask where you've been when you return from a day of fishing on the Chattooga, the correct answer is, "I don't believe I said."

A colorful Chattooga River rainbow.

Flies to Use (continued)

Nymphs & Wet Flies: #14-16 Y2K Bug, #14-16 Glo Egg, #14-16 San Juan Worm, #12-20 Prince Nymph, #12-20 Hare's Ear Nymph, #12-16 Zug Bug, #8-20 Pheasant Tail, #16-18 Grey Caddis Pupa, #18-22 Midge Pupa, #16-20 Black Stonefly Nymph, #14-16 Yellow Stonefly Nymph, #4-8 Golden Stonefly Nymph, #4-8 Black Stonefly Nymph, #12-14 Quill Gordon Nymph, #12-14 Cream Caddis Pupa, #12-14 Light Cahill Nymph, #12-14 Dun & Yellow Caddis Pupa, #8-14 March Brown Nymph, #14-18 Sulphur Nymph or Emerger, #8-10 Green Drake Nymph.

Streamers: #6-12 Krystal Bugger, #6-12 Woolly Bugger, #6-12 Muddler Minnow, #4-8 White Beadhead Flash Zonker, #4-8 Zonker, #4-10 Conehead Double Bunny, #6-8 Clouser Minnow, #6-10 Mickey Finn, #6-10 Black-nosed Dace.

Redeye bass/bream flies: #4-6 DP Popper, #4-6 DP Slider, #2-6 Kent's Stealth Bomber, #10 Carter's Rubber-legged Dragon, #1-2 Clouser Minnow, #1 Cowen's Coyote.

When to Fish

The best times of year to fish this river for trout are in the spring and fall when water temperatures are in that ideal 50 to 60 degree Fahrenheit range. Winter fishing can also be very productive when the midday sun warms the water and activates the chilly fish. For redeye bass and redbreasts, focus on the Reed Creek to Highway 76 area in the summer months.

Seasons & Limits

The Chattooga is a year-round fishery governed under general regulations. The portion of the river that forms the Georgia-South Carolina border can be fished with proper licensing from either state. However, tributaries can only be fished with licensing from the state through which they flow. Catch and release and artificials-only fishing are strictly enforced on the delayed harvest section of the river from November 1 through May 14. Of course, catch and release is always strongly encouraged.

Nearby Fly Fishing

The West Fork of the Chattooga, Warwoman Creek, Walnut Fork, and other Chattooga tributaries also offer smaller but less-pressured waters to chase all three salmonid species in Georgia.

Accommodations & Services

For dining and lodging, it's hard to beat the Dillard House in the nearby town of Dillard. Another good dining option is La Pachanga, a great place to eat Mexican food after a long day on the river. Reeves Ace Hardware has two locations, one in Dillard and one in Clayton, and both carry a good selection of flies and fly tackle, along with waders and wading boots. Check the U.S. Geological Survey's Chattooga flow gauge online—2.2 feet and lower on the gauge height is best for fishing and safe wading.

Helpful Web Sites

RabunTU.com
NGTO.org
GoFishGeorgia.com

Rating

This is the original Wild and Scenic River—not just in Georgia, but in the entire country. Mix amazing scenery, a wide variety of plant and wildlife, and a well-managed river and you get a perfect 10 out of 10.

Appalachian Autumn by Tom Landreth.

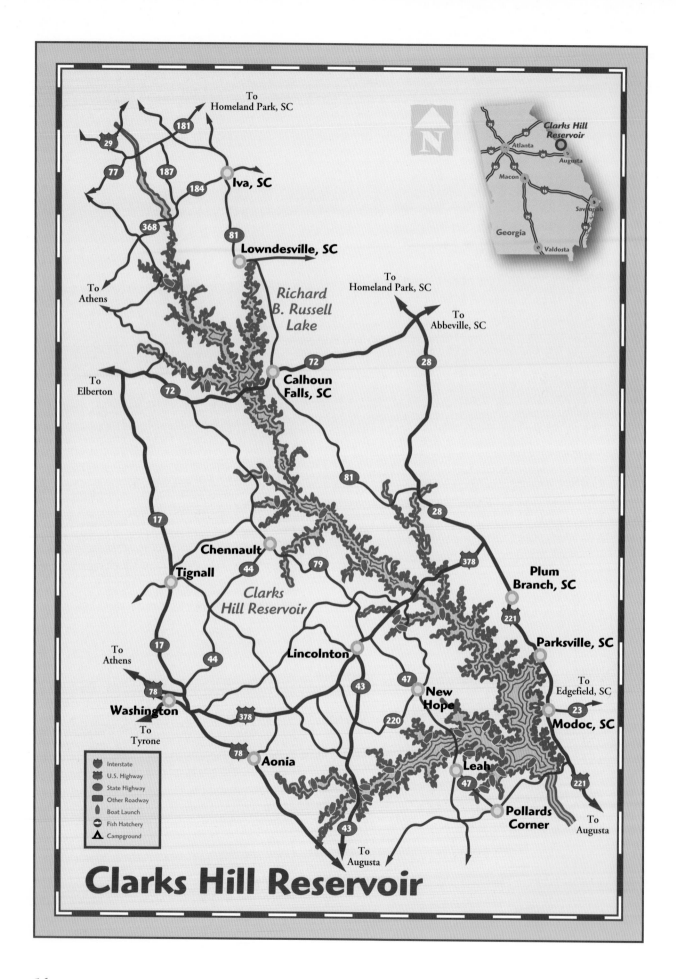

Clarks Hill Reservoir

Clarks Hill Reservoir

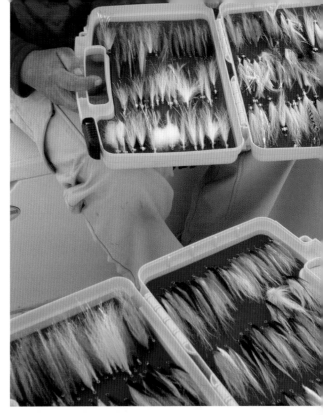

If you're from South Carolina, you'll call this huge 71,535-acre reservoir J. Strom Thurmond Lake. But here in Georgia, it's known as Clarks Hill. And from shoreline to shoreline, there may not be a better fishery in Georgia for pursuing hybrids and stripers on the fly.

In the winter months, the hybrids, stripers, and largemouth bass can be found mixed together in the morning chasing threadfin shad and blueback herring. These fish will be in the backs of creeks on the north end of the lake—east and north of the GA47 Bridge to be more specific. Later in the day, you'll generally find the "big three" of Clarks Hill suspended anywhere from 10 to 15 feet below the surface.

By early spring, the largemouth bass are getting on bed and preparing to spawn. This presents a great opportunity for sight fishing. If you're dragging a fly over a bass bed and get hit, it will likely be the buck bass—or smaller male bass—reacting to protect

Having a good selection of baitfish patterns on hand is a good idea on Clarks Hill.

Bill Howle keeps an eye out for schooling fish.

Anglers taking off to enjoy a brisk early morning on Clarks Hill Reservoir.

Cowen's Coyote

the redd. Land and release this fish quickly and cast to the same spot again. If you get hit this time, it will likely be the big female looking for a meal.

Big hybrids, stripers, and largemouths school on blueback herring as big as six to eight inches long on the main lake points. However, this time of year the fish probably won't be mixed together. You may catch a mixed bag of hybrids and stripers on one point, then largemouth bass on the next point you fish.

The hot southern summer drives hybrids and stripers too deep to target with flies, but largemouth bass get in hydrilla beds and will run bait in the grass. When these fish push the bait above the grass line and into shallow water, they are easy targets for fly fishermen.

Anglers who rely on conventional tackle the rest of the year will readily pull out a fly rod in the fall. The reason for doing this is the tiny threadfin shad that hatched the prior spring. Simply put, nothing but a one- to two-inch-long fly can effectively match this baitfish, which will be the main dish for hybrids and stripers who chase threadfins in open water. These fish can be as selective as spring creek trout and matching the hatch will be crucial to success during this time. Seeing several acres of boiling morones isn't uncommon during the early morning hours of fall—times like those are as exciting as any for an angler with fly rod in hand.

Bill Howle strips a fly in hopes of connecting with a big striper.

Types of Fish
There are plenty of species to chase in this mammoth reservoir, but the top three for fly rodders are stripers, hybrid striped bass, and largemouth bass. Big crappies are in the lake, too.

Known Hatches
A mayfly hatch occurs on the lake in late spring, but the main forage here consists of blueback herring and threadfin shad.

Equipment to Use
Rods: 7-10 weight, 9 to 10 feet in length.
Reels: Standard disc drag (a large-arbor reel is a good choice here).
Lines: Floating weight-forward to match rod weight, intermediate lines, 350-450 grain sinking lines.
Leaders: 7- to 9-foot leaders for floating lines, 4- to 6-foot leaders of 16- or 20-pound test for sinking lines.
Wading: If you have access to the back of a cove when the fish are there in the fall, you could wade or stalk the bank. For all other scenarios, a boat is needed.

Flies to Use
Surface Flies: #4-2/0 Blados's Crease Fly, #1/0-2/0 pencil popper.

Subsurface Flies: #4-2 Cowen's Somethin' Else, #1/0 Cowen's Baitfish, #4/0 Cowen's Magnum Baitfish, #1 Cowen's Coyote, #2/0-2 Clouser Minnow, #2-8 Chocklett's Gummy Minnow.

When to Fish
Summer is the only season not suited for fly anglers. Fall is really the best time for throwing small flies to match the threadfin shad. Winter and spring can be great, as well.

Seasons & Limits
This lake is open all year and falls under general regulations. A reciprocal agreement between Georgia and South Carolina allows someone with either license to fish the entire lake (except for flowing creeks feeding the lake). See GoFishGeorgia.com for all the details.

Nearby Fly Fishing
The Savannah River running through Augusta offers a smorgasbord of fly fishing opportunities.

Accommodations & Services
There are plenty of guides servicing the lake and a fly shop, Rivers & Glen Trading Company, in Augusta.

Helpful Web Sites
Clarks Hill fishing report:
GON.com/page.php?id=64

Rating
Clarks Hill is a big fish lake that can easily be a 9 out of 10.

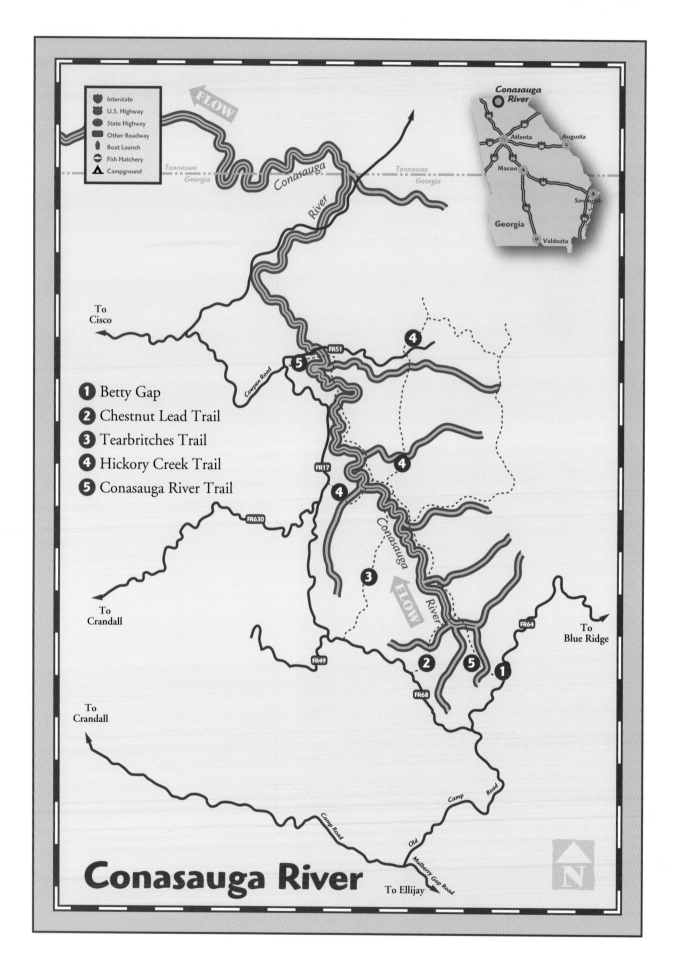

Legend:
- Interstate
- U.S. Highway
- State Highway
- Other Roadway
- Boat Launch
- Fish Hatchery
- Campground

FLOW

Conasauga River

Tennessee
Georgia

Tennessee
Georgia

Conasauga River

Atlanta

Augusta

Macon

Georgia

Savannah

Valdosta

To Cisco

FR51

5

4

Cowpen Road

1 Betty Gap
2 Chestnut Lead Trail
3 Tearbritches Trail
4 Hickory Creek Trail
5 Conasauga River Trail

FR17

4

4

FR630

3

Conasauga River

FLOW

To Crandall

FR49

2

5

1

FR64

To Blue Ridge

FR68

To Crandall

Camp Road

Camp Road

Old Mulberry Gap Road

Conasauga River

N

To Ellijay

Conasauga River

rouched on a high bank looking over the Conasauga River—which appears more as a creek than a river—an angler stares through a window of crystal clear water, hoping to see a sign of life and praying that life doesn't see him back. The mixture of surface foam and plaited currents flow over dark, ambiguous shapes that could be river rocks or, hopefully, the shadows of finning rainbows feeding in the current. Even with the aid of polarized sunglasses, though, it's still too close to call.

With a careless roll, one of the figures turns on its side to intercept a passing pupa washing downstream and simultaneously reveals the white of his underbelly. While the angler feels a sense of accomplishment for spotting this well-camouflaged creature, the battle has just begun. Getting to the point of presenting a fly, and presenting it well, to this fish that has watched tens of thousands of insects float by, will be no easy task. Its eyes are set in such a way as to spot anything coming from overhead, such as herons, kingfishers, or the ill-cast fly line. And should anything seem even a little bit off, this wild trout will develop an incurable case of lockjaw.

Types of Fish
Wild brown and rainbow trout.

Known Hatches
Small Dun Caddis, Blue-Winged Olive, Blue Quill Mayfly, Midges, Winter Black Stonefly, Quill Gordon Mayfly, Light Cahill Mayfly, Early Black Stonefly, Cream Caddis, Red Quill/Hendrickson, March Brown Mayfly, Yellow Stonefly, Golden Stonefly, Speckled Grey Caddis, Giant Black Stonefly, Sulphur Mayfly, Green Drake Mayfly, Coffin Fly (Green Drake Spinner).

Equipment to Use
Rods: 3-4 weight, 7 to 8½ feet in length.
Reels: Any reel with a mechanical drag.
Lines: Floating weight-forward or double-taper to match rod weight.
Leaders: 5X to 6X, 9 to 12 feet in length.
Wading: Waist-high waders are fine for most parts of the Conasauga, but chest waders are the best option.

Flies to Use
See the Southern Appalachian Freestone Hatch Chart to correctly match the hatch.

Dry Flies: #14-16 Black Ant Parachute, #12 Dave's Cricket, #6-10 Dave's Foam Hopper, #10-12 Yellow

Continued

The Conasauga is a small river, but is big on scenery.

An angler high sticks a run on the Conasauga.

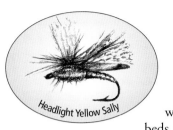

Headlight Yellow Sally

The "Connie," as its faithful affectionately call it, has very good numbers of wonderfully-marked wild trout from its spring source near Betty Gap—an area named after a widow who would sell meals and stays in warm beds to traveling loggers—to its marriage with Jacks River across the Tennessee state line. And this river would more appropriately be called a creek, at least across much of its flow through the western edge of the Cohutta Wilderness.

Like the rest of the lands inside the boundaries of the largest wilderness east of the Mississippi River, this area takes quite an effort to reach. One possible translation to English of the word Conasauga is "strong horse." If this is correct, it could have been a description of the forceful flows of the river during the spring rains. After hiking one of the five marked trails that either lead to or follow the Conasauga, however, you might share my sentiment of wanting a strong horse to carry you, your camping gear, and fly tackle.

Fishing this river in the spring and fall, like many other streams in Georgia, can be fantastic. But, there are plenty of other hikers and nature lovers traveling its trails this time of year. The Conasauga offers cool waters in the summer heat, too, but the water is typically low and as clear as clear can be. Not to mention, the crowds are in full force. If you want the real Conasauga experience, plan a trip with a few friends in the winter. The crowds are gone, the fish have seen fewer anglers, and there's no better time to be around a campfire.

Of course, if it ends up being one of those days when even crawling and stalking like a heron can't keep the fish from spooking, at least being on one's knees is a convenient posture for begging for mercy from these wary trout.

This pretty, wild rainbow fell for a Y2K Bug. Photo by Stephanie Cannon.

Flies to Use (continued)

Jacket, #14-20 Adams, #14-20 Adams Parachute, #16-18 Adams Irresistible, #16-20 Blue Quill #16-20 BWO, #18-22 Griffith's Gnat, #16-20 Elk Hair Caddis, #12-14 Quill Gordon, #14-16 Red Quill, #14-16 Hendrickson, #14 March Brown, #14 March Brown Parachute, #14-16 Yellow Stimulator, #12-18 Light Cahill, #12-18 Light Cahill Parachute, #14-18 Headlight Yellow Sally, #14-18 Sulphur Comparadun, #14-18 Cream Variant, #12-14 Blue Dun Parachute, #8-10 Green Drake, #8-10 Spent-wing Coffin Fly, #8-10 Parachute Coffin Fly, #20-22 Parachute Trico, #20-22 Black Poly Wing Spinner.

Nymphs: #14-16 San Juan Worm, #14-20 Prince Nymph, #14-20 Hare's Ear Nymph, #14-16 Zug Bug, #14-20 Pheasant Tail, #14-16 Tellico Nymph, #16-20 Lightning Bug, #16-20 Rainbow Warrior, #18-22 Zebra Midge, #18-22 Disco Midge, #18-22 WD-40, #18-22 Midge Pupa, #16-20 Black Stonefly Nymph, #14-16 Yellow Stonefly Nymph, #4-8 Golden Stonefly Nymph, #4-8 Black Stonefly Nymph, #12-14 Quill Gordon Nymph, #12-14 Light Cahill Nymph, #8-10 Green Drake Nymph.

Streamers: #10-14 Krystal Bugger, #10-14 Woolly Bugger, #10-14 Muddler Minnow, #8 White Beadhead Flash Zonker, #8 Zonker, #10 Mickey Finn, #10 Black-nosed Dace.

When to Fish

This river can provide good fishing year-round.

Seasons & Limits

The Conasauga is open for fishing all year, but from November 1 through the last Saturday in March, only artificial lures may be used. Night fishing is prohibited on the Conasauga.

Nearby Fly Fishing

Jacks River is on just the other side of the mountain from the Conasauga, but getting there is easier said than done.

Accommodations & Services

Highland Outfitters in Cartersville is the closest fly shop to the western side of the Cohutta Wilderness.

Helpful Information

HighlandOutfittersLLC.com
GoFishGeorgia.com

I highly recommend picking up a copy of the book *Hiking Trails of the Cohutta & Big Frog Wildernesses* by Tim Homan (Peachtree Publishers).

Rating

The Conasauga is a small, beautiful flow that can offer some very good fishing, making it an 8 out of 10.

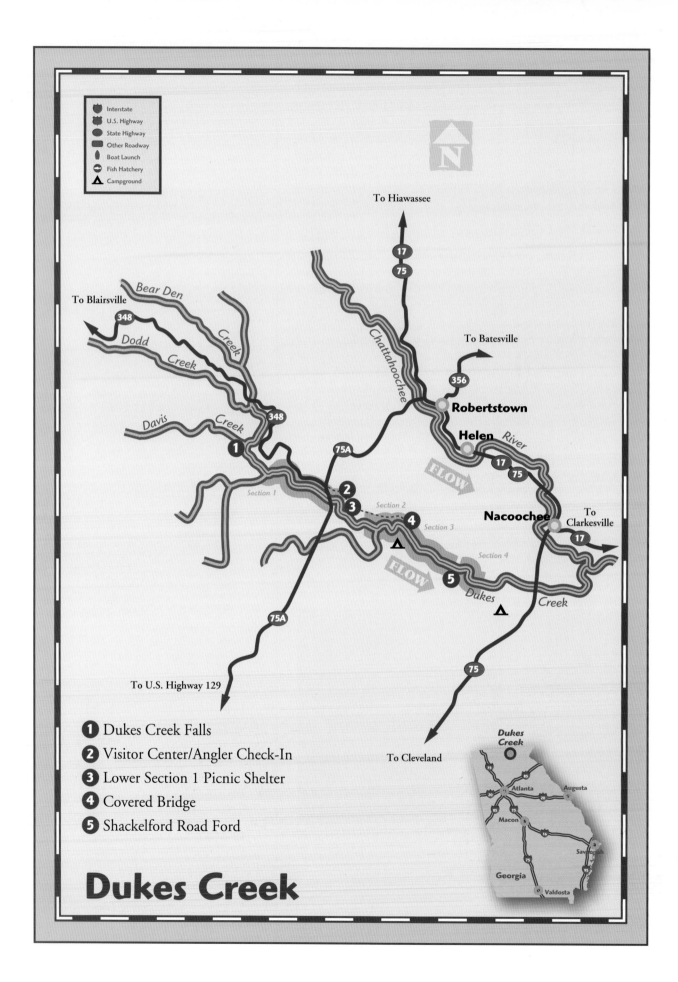

Legend:
- Interstate
- U.S. Highway
- State Highway
- Other Roadway
- Boat Launch
- Fish Hatchery
- ▲ Campground

1 Dukes Creek Falls
2 Visitor Center/Angler Check-In
3 Lower Section 1 Picnic Shelter
4 Covered Bridge
5 Shackelford Road Ford

Dukes Creek

To Hiawassee

To Blairsville

To Batesville

Robertstown

Helen

Nacoochee

To Clarkesville

To U.S. Highway 129

To Cleveland

Bear Den Creek
Dodd Creek
Davis Creek
Chattahoochee
River
FLOW
FLOW
Dukes Creek

Section 1
Section 2
Section 3
Section 4

348
75A
356
17
75

Georgia — Dukes Creek
Atlanta, Augusta, Macon, Savannah, Valdosta

Dukes Creek

The strike indicator drifts perfectly, floating at precisely the same speed as the surrounding bubbles bouncing downstream around boulders that cut a deep run where a notoriously huge Dukes Creek rainbow likely awaits. The strike indicator stalls ever so slightly and a 10-millisecond long argument between the idealistic and realistic sides of your brain is waged:

Is that a fish?
No, no, no—it's just the split shot snagging on a rock.
But what if it's a fish?
It's not. It's just your imagination.

Luckily, muscle memory takes over in the middle of the argument. The rod is raised, the line hand strips in the slack and a size 20 soft hackle pheasant tail pierces the lower jaw of one very large, and now very spooked, rainbow trout.

Your brain flashes to the scene in *Of Mice and Men* when Lennie Small gets frightened while stroking Curley's wife's hair and she ends up dead. You realize that, at least in this scenario, you are Curley's wife, the raging rainbow is Lennie and the hair that is being stroked entirely too hard is your 6X tippet. In an instant, "Lennie" leaps airborne towards a fallen tree and, like he has probably done

Types of Fish
The most frequent catch here is overhanging tree limbs. If you're a little bit good and a lot lucky, though, you can catch some very large rainbow and brown trout.

Known Hatches
There are rarely enough insects fluttering above the surface of Dukes Creek to cause fish to consistently rise. However, if you do see surface activity, it will likely be one of the following:

Small Dun Caddis, Blue-Winged Olive, Blue Quill Mayfly, Midges, Winter Black Stonefly, Quill Gordon Mayfly, Light Cahill Mayfly, Early Black Stonefly, Cream Caddis, Red Quill/Hendrickson, March Brown Mayfly, Yellow Stonefly, Golden Stonefly, Speckled Grey Caddis, Giant Black Stonefly, Sulphur Mayfly.

Equipment to Use
Rods: 4-6 weight, 7 to 8½ feet in length.
Reels: Standard disc drag (a disc drag really is a necessity here!).
Lines: Floating weight-forward or double-taper to match rod weight.
Leaders: Clear water - 5X-6X leaders, 9 to 15 feet in length; Stained water – 0X-3X leaders, 5 to 7 feet in length.
Wading: Hip- or waist-high waders are fine for this small stream unless it has been particularly rainy, then chest waders are in order. Wet-wading is also fine in the warmer months.

Pam McClure ties a secure knot in hopes of connecting with a Dukes Creek bruiser.

Dukes has heavy cover in most places, but a few openings in the foliage allow for some longer fly casting.

Soft Hackle Pheasant Tail

many times before, educates an angler on just how loud of a "PING" such a thin piece of monofilament can make as it cleanly breaks, creating a chasm between the ideal and the real.

More often than not, this is the reality of fishing the four-mile stretch of Dukes Creek that runs through the Smithgall Woods Conservation Area. This area became a part of history in 1828 when gold was first discovered here and, while the prospectors of America's first great Gold Rush made sure that no shiny speck remained, Dukes is now known to anglers as a treasure-trove of very large, very selective trout.

Because of its abundance of fish more than 20 inches in length, Dukes is easily one of the most challenging and exciting locales to fish for trout, and not just in Georgia. These fish have PhDs in fly identification and this small stream—less than 12 feet wide in most places—has tight casting quarters which presents anglers with either the perfect storm of fishing frustration or unbelievable reward.

Fooling the resident trout is difficult but not impossible. Keeping a Dr. Jekyll and Mr. Hyde mentality at Dukes is crucial to confronting its two faces. Because it is a headwater stream, it's typically crystal clear—meet Dr. Jekyll. But, if a lot of rain has fallen, the water will turn to chocolate and underwater visibility will decrease to mere inches—meet Mr. Hyde. To keep it as simple as possible, remember these two principles: when Dukes is low and clear, fish far and fine, and when it's muddy, fish big and ugly.

"Far and fine" means fishing flies size 18 and smaller tied to leaders as long as 15 feet and as light as 6X. Moving cautiously and wearing either dark-colored or camouflaged clothing are crucial under these conditions, too.

When Dukes is muddy, don't cancel your reservation! This is one of the few scenarios where the big fish feel safe enough to journey from the security of their holding spots. Swinging and stripping a big streamer tied to a 0X leader in the shallower, slower waters where anglers would normally wade can prove very effective.

A fine Dukes Creek rainbow trout. Photo by David Cannon.

Flies to Use

Dry Flies: #16-20 Elk Hair Caddis, #16-18 BWO, #16-22 Adams, #16-22 Adams Parachute, #16-20 Adams Irresistible, #18-22 Griffith's Gnat, #16-18 Blue Quill, #16-22 Light Cahill Dun, #16-22 Light Cahill Parachute, #14-18 Yellow Stimulator, #16-20 Royal Wulff, #16-20 Royal Trude.

Nymphs & Wet Flies: #14-16 Y2K Bug, #14-16 Glo Egg, #14-16 San Juan Worm, #12-20 Prince Nymph, #12-20 Hare's Ear Nymph, #12-16 Zug Bug, #8-20 Pheasant Tail, #16-18 Grey Caddis Pupa, #18-22 Midge Pupa, #16-20 Black Stonefly Nymph, #14-16 Yellow Stonefly Nymph, #4-8 Golden Stonefly Nymph, #4-8 Black Stonefly Nymph, #18-22 Disco Midge, #18-22 Zebra Midge, #16-22 Soft Hackle Wet, #16-22 Soft Hackle Pheasant Tail Nymph, #18-22 Lightning Bug, #18-22 Rainbow Warrior.

Streamers: #6-12 Krystal Bugger, #6-12 Woolly Bugger, #6-12 Muddler Minnow, #4-8 White Beadhead Flash Zonker, #4-8 Zonker, #4-10 Conehead Double Bunny, #6-8 Clouser Minnow, #6-10 Mickey Finn.

When to Fish

Rain or shine—especially rain. When you can get a reservation to fish the trophy section of Dukes, just go. You will either catch some beautiful fish or learn some valuable lessons!

Seasons & Limits

The trophy-managed section is open year-round on Saturdays, Sundays, and Wednesdays to anglers on a reservation basis that allows up to 15 anglers per session. Anglers must possess and fish only barbless hooks while in the area and must release all fish immediately after they are landed. Call (706) 878-3087 for reservations.

Nearby Fly Fishing

The headwaters of the Chattahoochee River and its tributaries are wonderful to explore. Unicoi Outfitters' trophy waters on the Chattahoochee, Nacoochee Bend, is five minutes away and home to large fish as is Waters Creek near Turner's Corner. The delayed harvest section of Smith Creek and the upper reaches of Dukes Creek are within a ten-minute drive of Smithgall Woods, as well.

Accommodations & Services

There are some very nice cabins on the grounds of Smithgall Woods that can be rented and will also allow the visitor to fish water that is off-limits to everyone else. The nearby alpine town of Helen offers a multitude of lodgings and restaurants to meet a variety of tastes. Helen is home to a great fly shop and outfitter, Unicoi Outfitters, which can suggest successful fly patterns or even set you up with a guide for your session.

Helpful Web Sites

NGTO.org
UnicoiOutfitters.com
GoFishGeorgia.com
SmithgallWoods.com
GAStateParks.org/info/smithgall/

Rating

A beautiful Southern Appalachian stream full of large, colorful, and challenging trout that can be fished by anyone with a license for the cost of a $3 park pass and a reservation make this location a perfect 10 out of 10.

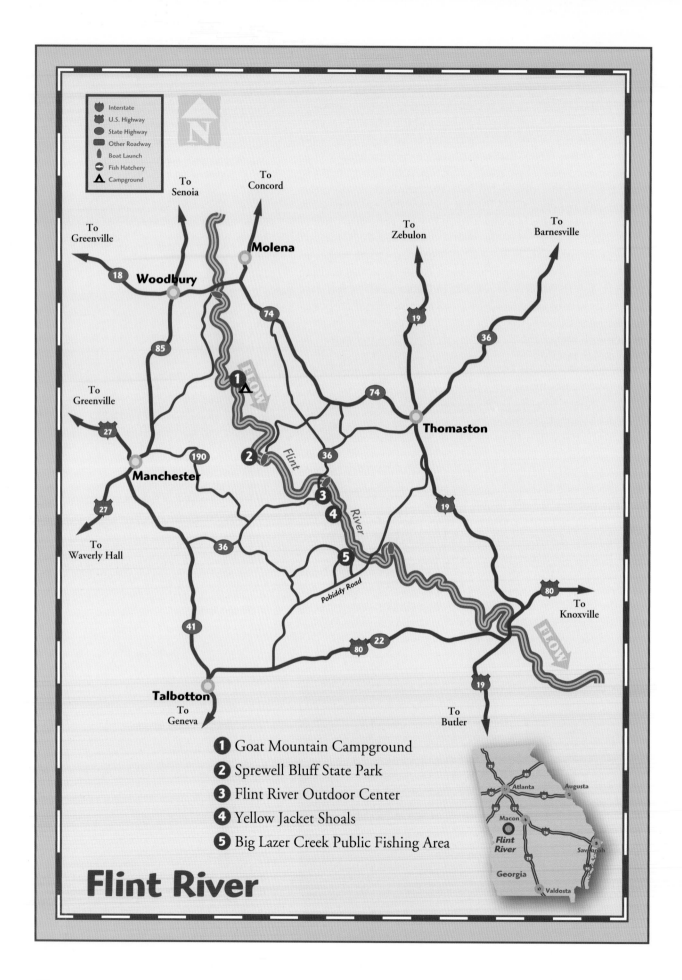

Legend
- Interstate
- U.S. Highway
- State Highway
- Other Roadway
- Boat Launch
- Fish Hatchery
- Campground

N

To Senoia

To Concord

To Greenville

To Zebulon

To Barnesville

Molena

18 Woodbury

74

19

85

1 FLOW

74

Thomaston

To Greenville

27

190

Flint

2

36

Manchester

3

19

27

4

River

To Waverly Hall

36

5

To Knoxville

80 FLOW

Pobiddy Road

41

80 22

19

Talbotton

To Geneva

To Butler

1 Goat Mountain Campground
2 Sprewell Bluff State Park
3 Flint River Outdoor Center
4 Yellow Jacket Shoals
5 Big Lazer Creek Public Fishing Area

Atlanta
Augusta
Macon
Flint River
Savannah
Georgia
Valdosta

Flint River

Flint River

Below the fall line (where the Piedmont meets the Coastal Plain) the Flint River is a wide, slow waterway filled with odd artifacts from native cultures and fascinating fossils including sharks' teeth and three near fully intact whale skeletons. This evidences that had this book been written in pre-historic times we would have had to include this area in the saltwater section.

Strangely enough, this river originates as a large group of underground springs contained by a mass of concrete under the north end of Atlanta Hartsfield-Jackson International Airport, the world's busiest hub for air travel (some Atlantans refer to it as Atlanta Hartsfield-Jackson-Crosby-Stills-and-Nash International Airport, in case you like a longer name for your airports).

From its origin, the Flint loses its urban image as it quickly widens, cuts through bluffs and flows over bedrock and boulders, dropping more than 400 feet over the course of about 80 miles and appearing as a mountain river that looks like a great place for trout or smallmouth. This swift, broken water that is commonplace above the fall line creates some great hiding places for one of Georgia's most intense game fishes, the shoal bass. And perhaps the best stretch of this river to target shoalies is the area from

Guide Kent Edmonds displays a Flint River shoal bass.

Ryan Whitelaw works a rocky run in hopes of hooking a shoal bass.

Ryan Whitelaw ties on a fly in the middle of the scenic Flint.

Kent's Stealth Bomber

Highway 18 between the towns of Woodbury and Molena downstream to just below Big Lazer Creek Wildlife Management Area in Talbot County, passing through Sprewell Bluff State Park near Thomaston along the way. More than four miles of the Flint are accessible by foot at Sprewell Bluff, but public access elsewhere along this river is limited, meaning a float trip is a great idea.

For many years, the shoal bass was regarded as a subspecies of another bass found in many of Georgia's rivers, the redeye. But that all changed in October of 1999 when the shoal bass was correctly classified and deemed to be more closely related to the spotted bass. As their name would imply, shoal bass love to hold in and around shoals and swift water.

When targeting shoal bass, think smallmouth bass or rainbow trout and stick to that braided water. But, don't just fish the obvious holding spots. Oftentimes, a shoalie will cram into a pothole amidst the shoals that isn't much bigger than he is. And while these fish were designed to thrive in and around shoals, slower, oxygen-rich water just below a set of shoals can prove productive, too. A Clouser Minnow, Woolly Bugger, or RLD stripped under the surface can entice a shoal bass. But as these fish are prone to attacking something making a ruckus on the surface, it's far more fun throwing a popper or Kent's Stealth Bomber, a fly designed by Flint River guide, tackle rep, and FFF Certified Casting Instructor Kent Edmonds.

Kent and his clients have been giving shoalies in the Highway 18 to Big Lazer stretch sore lips for years. Based on his experience, Kent says that fishing can be productive spring, summer, and fall but prime time occurs in April, May, and early June. No matter the time of year, the Flint is a river that all Georgia anglers will want to experience time and time again.

At Sprewell Bluff State Park, this middle Georgia river appears more as a north Georgia mountain flow.

A hellgramite is a large and tasty meal for a shoal bass.

Types of Fish

Largemouth bass, longnose gar, common carp, white bass, redbreasts, bluegill, and shellcracker (redear) can all be caught in this section of the Flint and stripers can be added to the list farther downstream. But, the star of the show is the native shoal bass.

Equipment to Use

Rods: 5-7 weight, 8-9 feet in length.
Reels: Standard disc drag.
Lines: Floating to match rod weight.
Leaders: 1X-4X leaders, 7-9 feet in length.
Wading: For most of the spring and fall, and all of summer, this warm-water fishery can be wet-waded. In cooler weather, opt for chest waders.

Flies to Use

Surface Flies: #2-6 Kent's Stealth Bomber, #4-6 DP Popper, #4-6 DP Slider, #4-8 Sneaky Pete, #1/0-2 Blados's Crease Fly, #2-4 Pencil Popper.

Subsurface Flies: #2-8 Woolly Bugger, #10 Carter's Rubber-legged Dragon, #1/0-2 Clouser Minnow, #2-8 Muddler Minnow, #1 Cowen's Coyote.

When to Fish

Targeting shoal bass in this section of the Flint can be good spring through fall, but prime time is April, May, and early June. The September and October months can also be great, but the fishing is much more "moody," says Kent Edmonds. Also note that this river will be unfishable after a heavy rain.

Seasons & Limits

In this year-round fishery, shoal bass less than 12 inches in length must be released immediately.

Helpful Web Sites

GeorgiaRiverFishing.com
FlyFishGA.com
GAStateParks.org/info/sprewell/

Rating

Because the Flint is immersed in Native American history and geological wonder, and as it is chock full o' shoal bass just looking to pounce on a fly, this water gets a perfect 10 out of 10.

Paul Puckett wades and casts in the marsh behind one of Georgia's eleven barrier islands. Photo by David Cannon

Georgia's Colonial Coast

As the crow flies, the Georgia coast is a short one. However, what is approximately 100 miles for the crow works out to be a maze of a few thousand miles of marsh grasses, oyster mounds, beaches, and tidal creeks for the angler.

Georgia's barrier islands, from north to south, are comprised of eleven islands: Tybee and Little Tybee, Wassaw, Ossabaw, St. Catherines, Sapelo, St. Simons and Little St. Simons, Sea Island, Jekyll, and Cumberland Island. Four of these islands, St. Simons and Little St. Simons, Sea Island and Jekyll Island are referred to as Georgia's Golden Isles either because of the golden sun that blankets this relatively unspoiled landscape or because of the wealthy families who have filled the exclusive resorts here since the Civil War.

Because of our coast's short length, the techniques for fishing from the north end of Tybee to the southern end of Cumberland Island are the same. For the sake of this book, the coast is broken up into two parts: the coast minus Cumberland Island and then Cumberland Island itself.

A real Georgia treasure is exploring Cumberland Island by foot and taking in all of its extraordinary qualities. Obtain a hiking map and enjoy that island. For the rest of the coast, launch your boat or hop in with one of our experienced fly fishing guides. The experience won't let you down.

Dupre's Spoonfly

A pelican searches the shoreline for feeding fish.

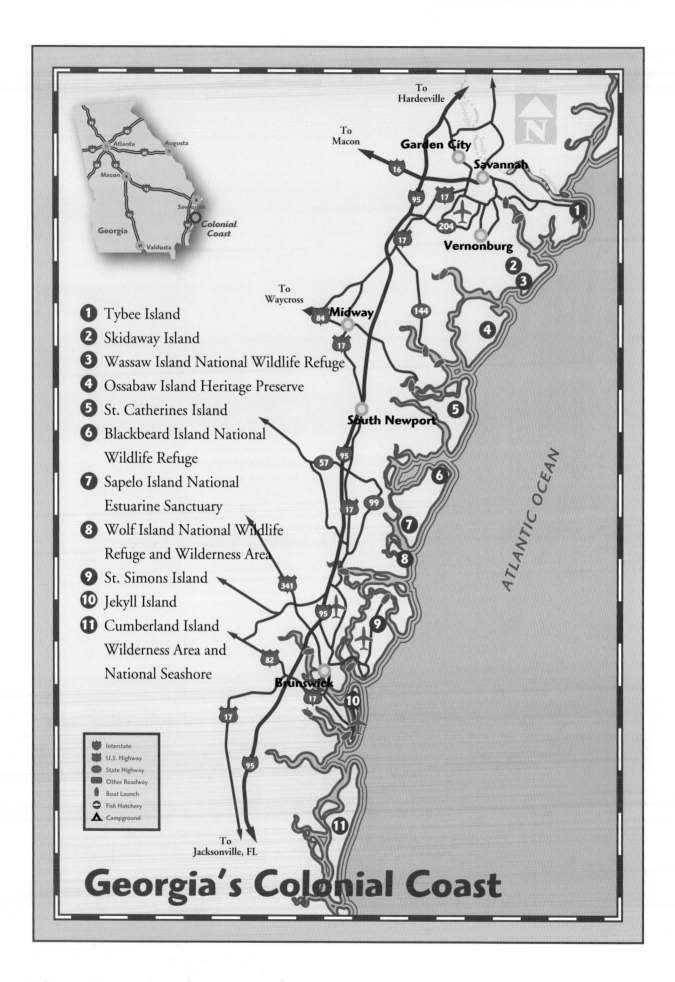

1 Tybee Island

2 Skidaway Island

3 Wassaw Island National Wildlife Refuge

4 Ossabaw Island Heritage Preserve

5 St. Catherines Island

6 Blackbeard Island National Wildlife Refuge

7 Sapelo Island National Estuarine Sanctuary

8 Wolf Island National Wildlife Refuge and Wilderness Area

9 St. Simons Island

10 Jekyll Island

11 Cumberland Island Wilderness Area and National Seashore

Interstate
U.S. Highway
State Highway
Other Roadway
Boat Launch
Fish Hatchery
Campground

Georgia's Colonial Coast

Georgia's Colonial Coast

Tybee Island to Golden Isles

For a long time, my unicorn was the redfish. No matter where I went, no matter how well I cast and fished, no matter who was poling the boat, I simply could not get a red to eat a fly. Reds haunted me to the point where I would have dreams—make that nightmares—about them and my inability to actually catch one.

In one such nightmare I spotted a tailing fish in a drainage ditch off the side of I-285 in Atlanta, and had nothing but the butt section of my 8-weight on me at the time. In another, my brother-in-law Matt was driving me around the Gulf Coast of Florida and tails were everywhere—in golf course ponds, roadside creeks, and even in those pink stucco fountains in the middle of shopping outlet centers. Every time I'd get ready to cast—from the roof of the van, of course—Matt would peel out, laughing as we left.

The last, and perhaps most disturbing of all, had me casting off of the bow of an experienced Georgia guide's skiff. He poled the boat perfectly and, for once in my dreams, I made the perfect cast to a huge red. Unbelievably, the fish took the fly! Deep into my backing it went, but I fought it perfectly. This time, the fish was mine.

When the giant drum was ready, I leaned off the side of the boat, grabbed him by the tail with one hand and under the belly

Types of Fish
Red drum, speckled trout, jack crevalle, ladyfish, black drum, tarpon, striped bass, and bluefish will be the primary targets, but don't miss the chance to cast to triple-tail, sheepshead, flounder, or a host of other characters just looking to survive in the salt.

Equipment to Use
Rods: 5-7 weights for speckled trout and ladyfish; 7-9 weights for redfish, bluefish, stripers and black drum; 10-12 weights for big jack crevalle and tarpon. All rods should be 9 to 10 feet in length.

Reels: A reel with a very good disc drag that is impervious to saltwater and sand.

Lines: Floating weight-forward and intermediate lines to match rod weight.

Leaders: 0X-2X leaders, 9 feet in length for trout, ladyfish and reds; leaders tapered to 20-pound test for jack crevalle, stripers, and black drum; leaders fashioned with a 30-pound test bite wire for bluefish; leaders tapered to a 16 or 20 pound line-class with a 60- or 80-pound shock tippet for tarpon.

Wading: Wet-wading the beach from mid-spring to mid-fall is an option, but chest waders should be worn during the cooler months. A boat or kayak is a must for fishing the marshes and creeks. However, some high-tide flats can be solid enough for wading.

Flies to Use
#2-2/0 Clouser Minnow, #1/0-3/0 Half-and-Half, #2/0 Dupre's Spoonfly, #2-4/0 Lefty's Deceiver, #1 Cowen's Coyote, #1/0 Cowen's Baitfish, #4/0 Cowen's Magnum Baitfish, #2-1/0 Cowen's Mullet, #1/0 Cave's Rattlin'

Continued

The Georgia Coast is largely unspoiled and uncrowded.

Tidal creeks can be a great place to search for trout and reds.

with the other and hoisted the 40-incher above my head in a show of victory. When I brought the beast back down to eye-level, however, I noticed that something wasn't quite right.

Just behind the gill plate, I saw a zipper. "Huh?" I mumbled. Setting the fish on the deck of the boat, I began to unzip the zipper and, to my horror, found that I had been duped by a striped bass dressed up in a redfish costume for some twisted aquatic version of Halloween.

Needless to say, I had to start suppressing late-night cravings of spicy foods. Fortunately for fly anglers visiting Georgia's Colonial Coast, there are enough redfish present in its waters to keep the prospect of such nightmares fairly low.

If you really want to increase your chances for catching a real live Georgia redfish, you have several options. Yes, these fish can be found all year. But like any other species, there are times when they are more actively feeding and more accessible to someone with a fly rod in hand. From September through February, chasing reds the last three to four hours of an outgoing tide and the first couple of hours of an incoming tide can be incredible. The cooler water has these fish schooling together to graze the mudflats and an angler that doesn't spook the school is almost always the angler who catches a lot of fish.

Low tide fishing in the summer months can also be amazing, particularly if you hit the tide right in the coolness of early mornings and late afternoons. From May through early October, fishing around the new and full moons can offer sight casting to tailing fish feeding in marsh grass. Without question, this is the most exciting way to pursue the red drum and one of fly fishing's many pinnacles.

If you catch so many reds that you get bored with them, or if you're like me and need a "Plan B," again, you have several options. Throwing poppers or Crease Flies in mornings and late evenings, especially in October, can result in a hook up with a speckled trout. The rest of the year, casting shrimp patterns or Clouser Minnows on intermediate or 350-grain sinking lines around structure can also entice a trout to take.

In June, July, and August, Spanish mackerel, small jack crevalles, and bluefish can be found off of bars on the ocean side and will readily hit a Clouser Minnow or Lefty's Deceiver.

There are also some huge jacks that run through Georgia waters in the hot summer months. Jacks up to 40 pounds have been caught on the fly in Georgia, so bring your 12-weight if this suits your fancy.

The ultimate is the mighty tarpon. Some huge tarpon swim in our waters from June through September but are very difficult to catch on the fly. Water that is usually at least slightly stained makes sight casting to these monsters difficult. And, because there is an abundance of baitfish, it's hard to entice them with an artificial.

Kyle Burrell displays a nice fly-caught Georgia redfish. Photo by Andy Meadows.

Flies to Use (continued)

Minnow, #4-2/0 Sea-Ducer, #2/0 Chocklett's Chubby Gummy Minnow, #4-3/0 Blados's Crease Fly, #2/0 Sea Habit Bucktail, #3/0 Shark/Cuda Fly, #4-1/0 Ultra Shrimp, #6-4 Walters' Action Crab, #6-4 Cowen's Crabbit, #6 Banded Shrimp, #2 Borski's Chernobyl Crab, #6 Dink, #6-4 Dorsy's Kwan, #2-2/0 Cave's Wobbler, #3/0-4/0 LeMay's Big Eye Tarpon, #1/0-3/0 Laid-Up Tarpon, #2/0-4/0 Banger, #2/0 Todd's Wiggle Minnow, #1/0 Merriman's Tarpon Toad.

When to Fish

There is almost always something biting year-round on Georgia's Colonial Coast. Some factors, such as large amounts of rain flushing freshwater across the flats, can slow the fishing significantly, however. Summer and fall are generally the best times to go after the target species, but warm winter days can also be epic.

Seasons & Limits

Open all year. Size limits determined by the targeted species. Visit GoFishGeorgia.com for a complete list of regulations.

Nearby Fly Fishing

Do you really need more than the entire Georgia coast? Greedy, greedy, greedy. If you do, Ski Rixen Pond on Jekyll Island is a good place to go after reds, trout, and flounder. Also, good fishing can be found on many of the freshwater bodies on Georgia's barrier islands.

Accommodations & Services

Several fly fishing guides such as Capt. Scott Owens, the crew at St. Simons Outfitters, Capt. Greg Hildreth, and Capt. Scott Wagner make their livelihood on these waters and all are quite good at it. There's no shortage of hotels and bed-and-breakfasts along the coast, and you can't beat a long weekend in Savannah or on Jekyll, St. Simons, or one of the other peaceful barrier islands.

Helpful Web Sites

saltwatertides.com/dynamic.dir/georgiasites.html
goldenislesflyfishing.com
flyfishgeorgia.com
stsimonsoutfitters.com
savannahfly.com

Rating

Georgia's Colonial Coast is full of variety, history, scenery, and solitude. All of this adds up to a 10 out of 10.

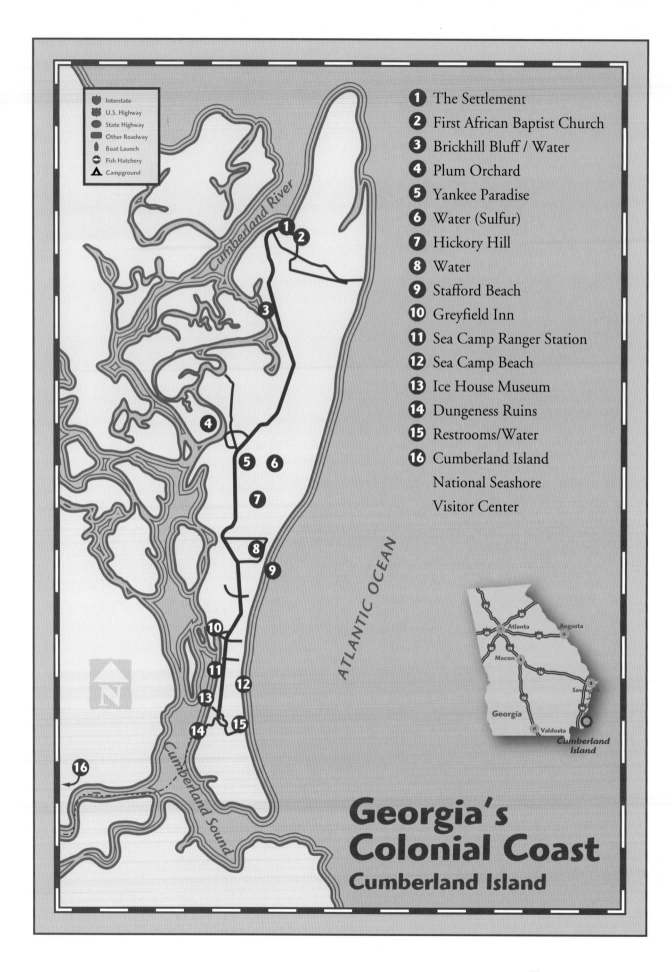

1 The Settlement
2 First African Baptist Church
3 Brickhill Bluff / Water
4 Plum Orchard
5 Yankee Paradise
6 Water (Sulfur)
7 Hickory Hill
8 Water
9 Stafford Beach
10 Greyfield Inn
11 Sea Camp Ranger Station
12 Sea Camp Beach
13 Ice House Museum
14 Dungeness Ruins
15 Restrooms/Water
16 Cumberland Island National Seashore Visitor Center

Interstate
U.S. Highway
State Highway
Other Roadway
Boat Launch
Fish Hatchery
Campground

Cumberland River

ATLANTIC OCEAN

Cumberland Sound

N

Georgia's Colonial Coast
Cumberland Island

Atlanta
Augusta
Macon
Savannah
Georgia
Valdosta
Cumberland Island

Georgia's Colonial Coast

Cumberland Island

If there is one destination in this book, or in the entire state for that matter, that simply can't be missed it is Cumberland Island.

Trying to describe this place to someone who has never been there is like trying to retell a Hemingway story. It's something that really has to be experienced to be fully appreciated. Simply put, Cumberland Island is 40 square miles of pure intrigue—an amazing confluence of history, adventure, and wildlife. Stepping off of the Cumberland Queen (the ferry) and onto the island is like stepping foot into a real-life land of make believe. Lush maritime forests full of sprawling live oaks, miles of unspoiled white-sand beaches traveled more by wild horses than humans, and the ruins of grand mansions built by some of the better-known families of the Gilded Age make for a bizarre yet beautiful setting.

There are only two options for staying on the island. The first is camping at one of Cumberland's designated sites, either developed or primitive. This option will cost you $4 per night per person and reservations can be made up to six months in advance by calling (912) 882-4335. Brickhill Bluff, one of Cumberland's four backcountry sites, is an eleven-mile hike from the landing

Poling around in a flats boat is the best way to sneak up on Georgia redfish in shallow water.

Jack Crevalle fight hard and will readily crush a fly placed in their path. Photo by Stephanie Cannon.

Guide Greg Hildreth poles David and Stephanie Cannon over a high-tide flat in search of redfish.

but, like the island itself, is worth the trouble of getting there. Sunsets at this site can be phenomenal and sighting manatees and dolphins in the Brickhill River below is a real possibility.

If camping doesn't suit your fancy, reservations can be made at the island's only lodging, the historic Greyfield Inn. A stay here includes various tours of the island, gourmet food, unlimited use of bicycles, and the greatest thing ever brought to the south—air conditioning. It stays booked, so reserve early.

Fishing the island is full of variety. If casting flies in the surf is your thing, the ocean side of Cumberland is one continuous stretch of beautiful beach—17 miles of it to be exact. Walking any length of this beach and casting Clouser Minnows, shrimp, or crab patterns into the breakers during the summer months can be productive.

On the other side of the island, exploring the vast marshes and web of tidal creeks could keep anyone busy for years. Redfish can be found on this side of the island year-round, particularly near oyster beds or at the mouths of creeks on a rising tide. And while the sight of a tailing redfish can really get an angler excited, nothing gets the heart pumping quite like a waking submarine heading to or from nearby Kings Bay Naval Submarine Base.

Between the ocean side and the inland side, there are some freshwater fishing opportunities. Bass and bream inhabit just about any body of freshwater you can find on the island, but so do alligators and snakes, so watch your step.

Aside from fishing, there are several other activities that should make your "to-do" list. Visiting the Dungeness Ruins should be tops on that list and stopping by any of the cemeteries or the First African Baptist Church, where John F. Kennedy Jr. and Carolyn Bessette were married, are great ways to experience Cumberland, as well.

Fishing Details
See Tybee Island to Golden Isles (pages 75, 77).

Accommodations & Services
Guides such as Capt. Scott Owens, the crew at St. Simons Outfitters and Capt. Greg Hildreth will all guide fly anglers around Cumberland. There's only one place to rent a room, the Greyfield Inn. If you want to go the cheap route, however, there are plenty of campsites across the island. Getting to the island, unless you have your own boat, is done via the Cumberland Queen ferry. Getting a reservation to ride the ferry is recommended and can be made by calling (912) 882-4335 or toll free at (887) 860-6787.

Helpful Web Sites
stmaryswelcome.com
saltwatertides.com/dynamic.dir/georgiasites.html
goldenislesflyfishing.com
flyfishgeorgia.com
stsimonsoutfitters.com
savannahfly.com

Rating
Cumberland Island is surrounded by great fishing opportunities and is a surreal location. If an 11 out of 10 were possible, that's what I would give it.

Spotted sea trout painting by Paul Puckett.

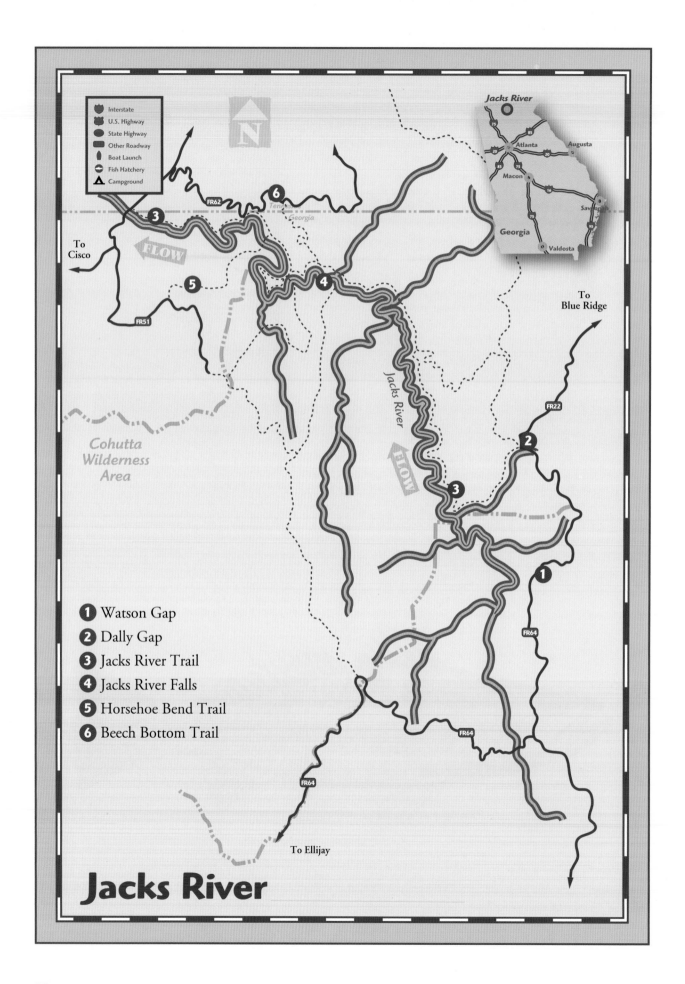

1 Watson Gap

2 Dally Gap

3 Jacks River Trail

4 Jacks River Falls

5 Horsehoe Bend Trail

6 Beech Bottom Trail

Jacks River

Jacks River

For many of us, our daily existence involves navigating rush-hour traffic, standing in lines, checking voicemails, emails, and the mailbox, and trying to keep it all together. Everywhere you look there are fences, guardrails and median walls, right-turn-only lanes, exit-only lanes, and dead-ends. Hurrying through our work week, being confined to four office walls—or a cubicle—and being a slave to a schedule can have even the most reserved among us shouting, "Serenity now!"

How many kids dream about this kind of life, of joining the rat race? At some point, though, ambitions and needs prioritize how we spend the bulk of our being. And the maze of life through which we scurry five days a week makes the remaining two days, and how we spend them, even more crucial to keeping that inner-kid alive.

If you really want to get away from it all, and I mean far away, and wake that youthful version of you, Jacks River in the Cohutta Wilderness is one of your best options. It's the biggest flow running through Cohutta and teems with wild trout—browns and rainbows.

The area is difficult to access—not because of a lack of trails, but because of the difficulty and length of them—and therefore is

Types of Fish
Wild rainbow and brown trout.

Known Hatches
Small Dun Caddis, Blue-Winged Olive, Blue Quill Mayfly, Midges, Winter Black Stonefly, Quill Gordon Mayfly, Light Cahill Mayfly, Early Black Stonefly, Cream Caddis, Red Quill/Hendrickson, March Brown Mayfly, Yellow Stonefly, Golden Stonefly, Speckled Grey Caddis, Giant Black Stonefly, Sulphur Mayfly, Green Drake Mayfly, Coffin Fly (Green Drake Spinner).

Equipment to Use
Rods: 3-4 weight, 8 to 9 feet in length.
Reels: Any reel with a mechanical drag.
Lines: Floating weight-forward or double-taper to match rod weight.
Leaders: 5X to 6X, 9 to 12 feet in length.
Wading: Jacks is pretty big water by Georgia standards. Chest waders are recommended.

Flies to Use
See the Southern Appalachian Freestone Hatch Chart to correctly match the hatch.

Dry Flies: #14-16 Black Ant Parachute, #12 Dave's Cricket, #6-10 Dave's Foam Hopper, #10-12 Yellow Jacket, #14-20 Adams, #14-20 Adams Parachute, #16-18 Adams Irresistible, #16-20 Blue Quill, #16-20 BWO, #18-22 Griffith's Gnat, #16-20 Elk Hair Caddis, #12-14 Quill Gordon, #14-16 Red Quill, #14-16 Hendrickson,

Continued

The author roll casts for Jacks River trout.

Jacks has a medium-sized flow with good opportunities for fish and a backcountry experience.

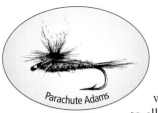
Parachute Adams

accessed more by hikers and less by anglers. Beech Bottom Trail, Rice Camp Trail, and the Penitentiary Branch Trail (named by the loggers of the early twentieth century who worked the area which was too remote to allow them to leave for their only day off, making them feel as if they were incarcerated) are the shortest and easiest of trails to access Jacks and the paralleling Jacks River Trail. If you want to check out Jacks River Falls, the most popular attraction in the Cohutta Wilderness, Beech Bottom Trail intersects the Jacks River Trail only about a half-mile upstream of it.

Jacks is typically gin clear and calls for the use of natural-looking imitations, or flies made more with fur and feather and absent of a lot of flash. Fishing dries and dry-dropper combos are the common way to fish, but don't forego tying on a streamer and hunting for a nice brown. They've been caught here up to nine pounds, but a more typical catch is in the 9- to 12-inch range.

When heading through Blue Ridge and towards the Jacks access points, your practical side may say that it makes more sense to stick to that area. "The Toccoa River and Blue Ridge Reservoir are right here," it whispers, "and Jones and Noontootla Creeks aren't too far, either." "No, let's go explore," says the kid in you. And just this once, let that side win. Go discover and enjoy an area where lanes and lights don't dictate which way to turn. Then again, if you're hearing two voices in your head, maybe you should get out of the city altogether.

David Cannon fights a fish near a popular access point.

Flies to Use (continued)

#14 March Brown, #14 March Brown Parachute, #14-16 Yellow Stimulator, #12-18 Light Cahill, #12-18 Light Cahill Parachute, #14-18 Sulphur Comparadun, #14-18 Cream Variant, #12-14 Blue Dun Parachute, #8-10 Green Drake, #8-10 Spent-wing Coffin Fly, #8-10 Parachute Coffin Fly, #20-22 Parachute Trico, #20-22 Black Poly Wing Spinner.

Nymphs: #14-16 San Juan Worm, #14-20 Prince Nymph, #14-20 Hare's Ear Nymph, #14-16 Zug Bug, #14-20 Pheasant Tail, #14-16 Tellico Nymph, #16-20 Lightning Bug, #16-20 Rainbow Warrior, #18-22 Zebra Midge, #18-22 Disco Midge, #18-22 WD-40, #18-22 Midge Pupa, #16-20 Black Stonefly Nymph, #14-16 Yellow Stonefly Nymph, #4-8 Golden Stonefly Nymph, #4-8 Black Stonefly Nymph, #12-14 Quill Gordon Nymph, #12-14 Light Cahill Nymph, #8-10 Green Drake Nymph.

Streamers: #10-14 Krystal Bugger, #10-14 Woolly Bugger, #10-14 Muddler Minnow, #8 White Beadhead Flash Zonker, #8 Zonker, #10 Mickey Finn, #10 Black-nosed Dace.

When to Fish

When the spring rains have subsided and the water is still flowing high, but clear. This usually centers around the month of May.

Seasons & Limits

Jacks River and its tributaries are all seasonal trout streams (open from the last Saturday in March through October 31) under general regulations.

Nearby Fly Fishing

The Conasauga River and its feeder creeks also lie within the Cohutta Wilderness, but "nearby" is a relative term when you have to hike over mountains to get to it.

Accommodations & Services

Unicoi Outfitters in Blue Ridge is the most convenient fly shop to the eastern side of the Cohutta Wilderness.

Helpful Information

UnicoiOutfitters.com
GoFishGeorgia.com

I highly recommend picking up a copy of the book *Hiking Trails of the Cohutta & Big Frog Wildernesses* by Tim Homan (Peachtree Publishers).

Rating

Jacks is difficult to access but offers the ambitious angler solitude and serenity. I give it a 7 of 10.

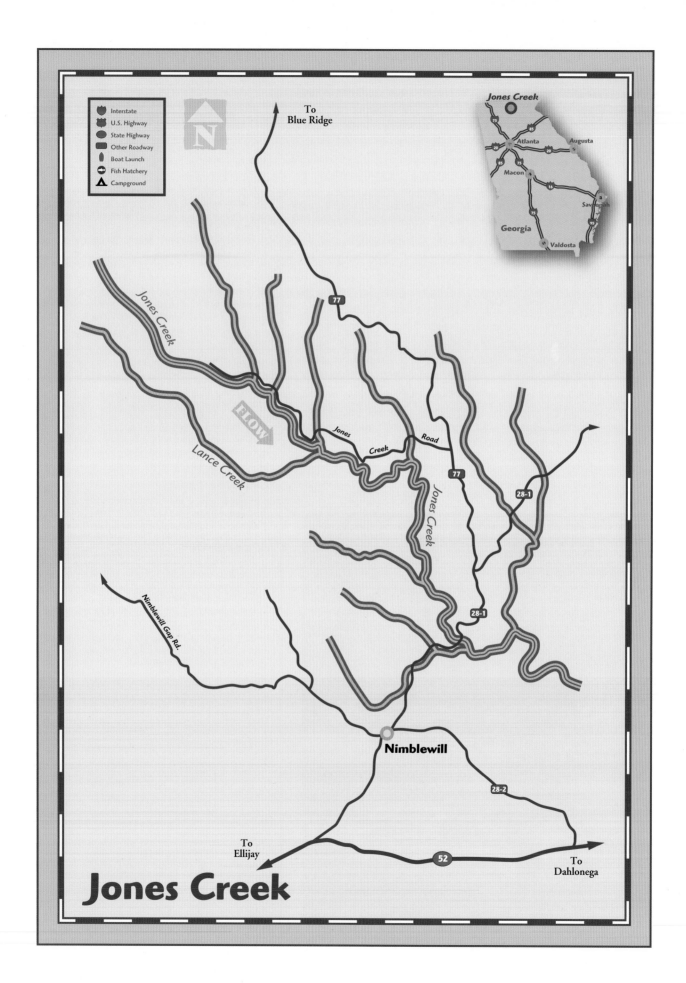

Jones Creek

Legend:
- Interstate
- U.S. Highway
- State Highway
- Other Roadway
- Boat Launch
- Fish Hatchery
- Campground

N

To Blue Ridge

Jones Creek

Lance Creek

FLOW

Jones Creek Road

Jones Creek

77

28-1

28-1

Nimblewill Gap Rd.

Nimblewill

28-2

To Ellijay

52

To Dahlonega

Jones Creek

Georgia
Atlanta
Augusta
Macon
Savannah
Valdosta

Jones Creek

In the Harrison Ford movie *Clear and Present Danger*, actor Raymond Cruz plays one of the more memorable characters, special ops sniper Domingo Chavez. In an unforgettable scene where the snipers are being tested, Chavez sneaks within feet of his commanding officers and hits the bulls-eye on target after target while they are trying to spot him with binoculars. Covered in a camouflage suit made of surrounding grasses, Chavez even manages to stop for lunch during the testing and uses the wrapper from his quarter-pounder (with cheese) as a decoy to distract his pursuers.

If you're brave enough to head to Jones Creek, you'll need all the stealth, skill, and even camouflage of Chavez, and a little luck, too. This small tributary of the Etowah River is on the other side of the mountain from Noontootla Creek and it's as odd a stream as we have in Georgia. It's particularly peculiar because it's managed as a wild brown trout fishery, which means that it is an unusually difficult creek.

Salmo trutta, or the brown trout, is infamous for its efficiency, wariness, and stubborn attitude. Kyle Burrell, a native of Rabun County in northeast Georgia, guide on the Chattahoochee in Atlanta (another great brown trout fishery), and environmental

Types of Fish
Beautiful, maddening, frustrating, and spooky wild brown trout.

Known Hatches
Small Dun Caddis, Blue-Winged Olive, Blue Quill Mayfly, Midges, Winter Black Stonefly, Quill Gordon Mayfly, Light Cahill Mayfly, Early Black Stonefly, Cream Caddis, Red Quill/Hendrickson, March Brown Mayfly, Yellow Stonefly, Golden Stonefly, Speckled Grey Caddis, Giant Black Stonefly, Sulphur Mayfly, Green Drake Mayfly, Coffin Fly (Green Drake Spinner).

Equipment to Use
Rods: 3-4 weight, 6 to 8 feet in length.
Reels: Any mechanical reel will do.
Lines: Floating weight-forward or double-taper to match rod weight.
Leaders: 5X to 6X, 9 feet in length.
Wading: Hip waders suffice and wet-wading works when it's warm.

Flies to Use
See the Southern Appalachian Freestone Hatch Chart to correctly match the hatch.

Dry Flies: #14-16 Black Ant Parachute, #12 Dave's Cricket, #6-10 Dave's Foam Hopper, #10-12 Yellow Jacket, #14-20 Adams, #14-20 Adams Parachute, #16-20 Blue Quill #16-20 BWO, #18-22 Griffith's Gnat, #16-20 Elk Hair Caddis, #12-14 Quill Gordon, #14-16 Red

Continued

Matt Anderson sits high above Jones Creek in an attempt to spot a feeding brown trout. Photo by David Cannon.

An angler fishes a plunge pool in search of a brown.

Golden Stonefly Nymph

scientist told me about his graduate thesis which was on the movement of wild browns in the Chattooga watershed. Kyle affixed radio transmitters to fish he caught that were more than 13 inches and tracked them for an entire year.

What he observed was pretty amazing. These fish barely moved and were extremely nocturnal. They generally stayed behind the same rock or tucked beneath the same undercut all day long. From last light, throughout the night, and until first light of the next day, however, they would come out of their holding spots and feed. And while one fish moved more than four miles to spawn, they rarely moved outside an area covering 150 feet during their nighttime grazing.

Though Kyle's study was on browns in the Chattooga, one could assume that the same holds true for wild browns in other streams. Trout Unlimited has placed several stream structures along the length of Jones Creek to increase holding areas for the occupying browns, and these areas—along with root wads, boulders, and undercut banks—are usually the best spots for concentrating your fishing efforts. You'll snag and lose a few more flies while focusing on these areas, but it will probably be worth it.

Other studies have shown that browns will only move a few inches to suck in prey, unlike rainbows that will move several feet to snatch a passing nymph. So you'll have to drift your fly at the correct depth and put it right on their nose in order to make them eat. Then again, they may not like what you've tied on and watch it pass by.

Focus your efforts in the early mornings, late evenings, on cloudy days, and when rain puts a stain on the water and watch your catch rates go way up.

The average Jones Creek brown trout may only be seven or eight inches, but any fish caught here should be considered a real victory.

Flies to Use (continued)

Quill, #14-16 Hendrickson, #14 March Brown, #14 March Brown Parachute, #14-16 Yellow Stimulator, #12-18 Light Cahill, #12-18 Light Cahill Parachute, #14-18 Sulphur Comparadun, #14-18 Cream Variant, #12-14 Blue Dun Parachute, #8-10 Green Drake, #8-10 Spent-wing Coffin Fly, #8-10 Parachute Coffin Fly, #20-22 Parachute Trico, #20-22 Black Poly Wing Spinner.

Nymphs: #14-16 Y2K Bug, #14-16 Glo Egg, #14-16 San Juan Worm, #14-20 Prince Nymph, #14-20 Hare's Ear Nymph, #14-16 Zug Bug, #14-20 Pheasant Tail, #16-20 Lightning Bug, #16-20 Rainbow Warrior, #18-22 Zebra Midge, #18-22 Disco Midge, #18-22 WD-40, #18-22 Midge Pupa, #16-20 Black Stonefly Nymph, #14-16 Yellow Stonefly Nymph, #4-8 Golden Stonefly Nymph, #4-8 Black Stonefly Nymph, #12-14 Quill Gordon Nymph, #12-14 Light Cahill Nymph, #8-10 Green Drake Nymph.

Streamers: #10-14 Krystal Bugger, #10-14 Woolly Bugger, #10-14 Muddler Minnow, #8 White Beadhead Flash Zonker, #8 Zonker, #10 Clouser Minnow, #10 Mickey Finn, #10 Black-nosed Dace.

When to Fish

The best times to fish here are in the early morning and late evening hours, on cloudy days and when rain has stained the water.

Seasons & Limits

Jones is a seasonal stream that opens on the last Saturday of March and closes October 31. It is a special regulation stream restricted to artificial lures.

Nearby Fly Fishing

Noontootla Creek, trophy-managed Noontootla Creek Farms, the Toccoa delayed harvest, the Toccoa tailwater, and Blue Ridge Reservoir are all within a 30-minute drive.

Accommodations & Services

Unicoi Outfitters in Blue Ridge is the closest fly shop to Jones and it can be a great idea to hire a guide from there for your first trip to this challenging stream. There are cabins for rent in the Aska Adventure area between Jones and the town of Blue Ridge. And Blue Ridge also has plenty of lodging and dining spots.

Helpful Web Sites

UnicoiOutfitters.com
GoFishGeorgia.com

Rating

The rating of this stream is very subjective. For a highly skilled and stealthy angler who really loves the small stream experience, it can be a 9 or even a 10. For a gawky 6'4" guy like me, it's a 7.

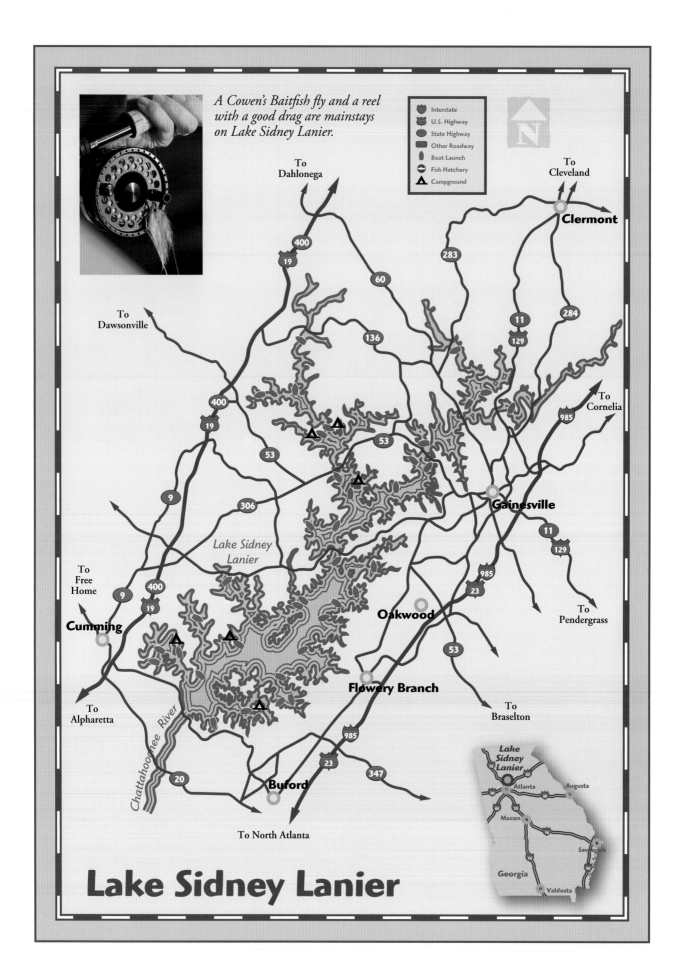

A Cowen's Baitfish fly and a reel with a good drag are mainstays on Lake Sidney Lanier.

Interstate
U.S. Highway
State Highway
Other Roadway
Boat Launch
Fish Hatchery
Campground

N

To Dahlonega

To Cleveland

Clermont

283

400

19

60

11

129

284

To Dawsonville

136

400

19

To Cornelia

985

53

53

9

306

Gainesville

11

129

Lake Sidney Lanier

985

To Free Home

9

400

19

23

To Pendergrass

Cumming

Oakwood

53

To Alpharetta

Flowery Branch

To Braselton

985

Chattahoochee River

23

20

347

Buford

To North Atlanta

Lake Sidney Lanier

Atlanta

Augusta

Macon

Savannah

Georgia

Valdosta

Lake Sidney Lanier

Lake Sidney Lanier

On a still, grey, and intensely cold morning on Georgia's largest lake, there's only one thing thicker than the anticipation of seeing feeding stripers on the surface, and that's the Brooklyn accent that breaks the silence. "What time is it, ten afta seven? Give it twenty more minutes. They'll show."

The thought occurs that no one could know precisely what time a school of big stripers are going to locate a school of shad, surround them, force them to pack together like sardines in a tin can and then drive them to the surface. That notion quickly dissipates as you remember that you're in Henry Cowen's boat, on Henry Cowen's home water, and fishing with Henry Cowen's nationally renowned flies designed specifically for these Lanier linesides.

Twenty minutes later, the seagulls that come to roost at Lanier for the winter start to move as a splash 100 yards behind the boat sounds. Then three, no, four more fish surface. The 225 horsepower Honda comes to life and your pulse redlines as Henry advises, "Strip out some fly line and get ready." The boat is swung perfectly into position just as your last false casts transfers into the delivery. Strip . . . strip . . . strip . . . "There he is!" And the marauding morone dives deep below with strength that rivals any of the Volkswagen-size catfish patrolling Buford Dam.

Clouser Minnows tied in a variety of sizes and colors should accompany any Lake Sidney Lanier fly angler. Photo by David Cannon.

A large fly-caught Lanier striped bass nears the boat.

Pat Gorman displays a nice spotted bass caught on Lake Sidney Lanier. Photo by David Cannon.

Cowen's Baitfish

The Georgia Department of Natural Resources first placed stripers in the 38,000-acre Lake Sidney Lanier in the early 1970s to control the threadfin shad. A great side effect of that was the creation of a saltwater-like fishery perfectly suited for the fly rodder for three of the four seasons.

In December, the gulls serve as aerial guides as to the location of schools of stripers and the action can get absolutely crazy. When schools aren't making a ruckus on the surface, cast to points on the main river channels—the Chattahoochee and Chestatee.

From about New Year's Day through the month of March, the stripers will be focused on tiny threadfin shad—only one or two inches long—and by early spring will be hitting them on red-clay banks warmed by the afternoon sun. This time of year, a small baitfish pattern with a lot of movement, like Cowen's Somethin' Else, will be effective when tied to light (12-pound test) leaders.

In late spring the stripers move upriver to spawn and when they return to the lake, they are hungry. The fish can be found staging on points on the main lake channels pre- and post-spawn. The shad spawn also occurs during this time of year and on any given morning, a 30-minute window may open when stripers and spots voraciously feed off of rocky banks where the shad eggs can stick. They also target huge seven- to eight-inch gizzard shad, which can be matched with Cowen's Magnum Baitfish, at first and last light in April.

Stripers are generally too deep to target on the fly in the summer, but by mid-October, the topwater action heats up again. By the end of the month, literally hundreds of fish will be crashing blueback herring from roughly 3:00 PM until dark when conditions are right.

The striper fishing here can be unbelievable, but this is also a world-class spotted bass fishery. A client of Henry's boated an IGFA line class record spot in 2008 and many fish in the four-pound range are caught on the fly every year. If that doesn't make you want to get out on "the pond" nothing will.

Renowned fly designer, writer, and guide Henry Cowen fights yet another large Lanier lineside. Photo by David Cannon.

Types of Fish
The fishing for largemouth bass, carp, bluegill, crappie, and even walleye is good in Lake Sidney Lanier. However, this is a world-class spotted bass fishery and an excellent place for chasing stripers on the fly.

Known Hatches
The main forage for spots and stripers here are threadfin shad and blueback herring. Huge gizzard shad are also on the menu in the spring.

Equipment to Use
Rods: 7-10 weight, 9 to 10 feet in length.

Reels: Standard disc drag (A large-arbor reel is helpful when fighting larger stripers).

Lines: Floating weight-forward to match rod weight, Intermediate lines, 350-450 grain sinking lines.

Leaders: 7- to 9-foot leaders for floating lines, 4- to 6-foot leaders of 16- or 20-pound test for sinking lines (except in the spring when it needs to be tapered down to 12-pound test).

Wading: When the fish are feeding in the backs of coves in the winter months, wading is a possibility with access available at several parks on Lanier. Chest waders are recommended for this type of fishing as is a stripping basket to help manage your fly line. For all other scenarios, a boat is a must-have item.

Flies to Use
Surface Flies: #1/0-2/0 Blados's Crease Fly, #1/0-2/0 pencil popper.

Subsurface Flies: #4-2 Cowen's Somethin' Else, #1/0 Cowen's Baitfish, #4/0 Cowen's Magnum Baitfish, #1 Cowen's Coyote, #2/0-2 Clouser Minnow, #2-8 Chocklett's Gummy Minnow.

When to Fish
For fly anglers, any time except summertime can be good. For striped bass fishing, overcast days are desired over sunny days.

Seasons & Limits
All fish can be targeted in Lake Sidney Lanier year-round. Up to 10 black basses, 15 stripers (only 2 fish over 22"), 30 crappie, 50 bream, and 8 walleye can be kept legally. However, catch and release is encouraged, particularly of spots, largemouths, and stripers.

Nearby Fly Fishing
The Chattahoochee River upstream of the lake and the tailwater coming out of the lake are both excellent waters for pursuing trout and shoal bass.

Accommodations & Services
There's no shortage of accommodations on Lake Sidney Lanier, whether it's lodging, marinas, dining, or guides you're after.

Helpful Web Sites
henrycowenflyfishing.com
GON.com/page.php?id=70

Rating
When the striper bite is on, Lake Sidney Lanier is at least a 9 out of 10.

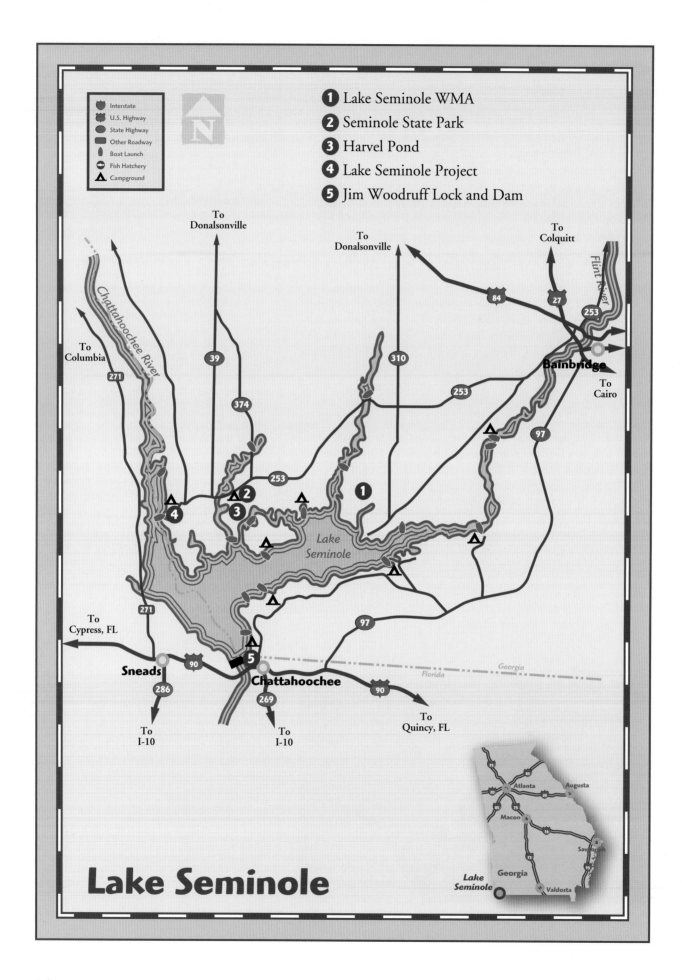

1 Lake Seminole WMA
2 Seminole State Park
3 Harvel Pond
4 Lake Seminole Project
5 Jim Woodruff Lock and Dam

Legend:
Interstate
U.S. Highway
State Highway
Other Roadway
Boat Launch
Fish Hatchery
Campground

To Donalsonville
To Donalsonville
To Colquitt
To Columbia
To Cairo
To Cypress, FL
To I-10
To I-10
To Quincy, FL

Chattahoochee River
Flint River
Lake Seminole

Sneads
Chattahoochee
Bainbridge

Georgia
Florida

271
39
374
253
310
84
27
253
253
97
97
90
271
286
269
90

Atlanta
Augusta
Macon
Savannah
Valdosta
Georgia
Lake Seminole

Lake Seminole

Lake Seminole

Close your eyes for a few seconds and envision the perfect bass lake. You have one of those new largemouth-specific fly rods in one hand and a box filled with big, meaty bass flies in the other. What do you want this bass paradise to look like?

Does it have standing timber near a cool spring upwelling? Are stumps lining the banks with more submerged just below the water line? Are there huge lily pads floating over flats with just enough of a path between them to hop that foam frog? What about a few skinny creeks running into the main lake that look inconspicuous, but upon closer inspection open up to reveal new worlds of shallow, fertile backwater?

Well, the dream lake is a reality. And the same fishing license that allows you to chase stripers on the fly at Lake Sidney Lanier, smallmouth in Blue Ridge Reservoir, and redfish on the Georgia coast grants you access to most of the 37,500 acres of bass-topia that is Lake Seminole ("most" because there is an area of Seminole that requires a Florida license).

It's no surprise that Seminole is such a great lake. It's the sum of two great parts: the Chattahoochee River and the Flint River. And because it lies on the Coastal Plain, straddling the Georgia-Florida-Alabama state lines, it is shallow. The average depth of

Types of Fish
Largemouth bass, striped bass, white bass and hybrid striped bass, bream, crappie, longnose gar, pickerel, and even shoal bass in the upper lake river arms.

Known Hatches
There is an epic mayfly hatch in June. For the rest of the year, the bass like to feed on dragon and damselflies, shad, bream, frogs, and snakes.

Equipment to Use
Rods: 8-10 weight rods, 7 feet 11 inches to 9 feet in length (the heavier, the better as you'll need some backbone to pull these big fish out of the vegetation and away from stumps).

Reels: A reel with a good disc drag is a true necessity here.

Lines: Floating and intermediate lines matched to rod weight.

Leaders: 7½-foot leaders tapered to 15-pound test for use with floating lines; 4'-6' leaders of straight 20-pound test for use with intermediate lines.

Wading: A boat is needed here unless you really like being that close to alligators.

Flies to Use
Surface Flies: #4-6 DP Popper, #4-6 DP Slider, #10 Deer Hair Popper, #6 Dahlberg Diver, #2-6 Swimming Frog, #2 Deer Hair Mouse Rat, #1/0 Foammaster Frog,

Continued

Guide Mike Sloan (left) and the author fish the lily pads in search of a big Seminole largemouth.

The author makes the first cast of the day on one of Georgia's best bass lakes.

DP Slider

this lake is 10 to 12 feet—perfect for fly fishing.

Because of its geographic location, summers are *Hot* with a capital 'H' and the fishing can be tough. However, the other side of that coin is that winter fishing can be fantastic. On the southern end of the lake, some bass actually get on the bed in mid-January. For the following six weeks or so, the spawn continues up the lake and the fish stay shallow through March, April, and a good part of May. The cooling fall weather brings the bass back to the shallows, making them prime targets for fly anglers all over again.

Just when the weather gets a little too hot to keep the bass shallow, something great happens—a mayfly hatch of biblical proportions. When this hatch occurs, the "willow bugs," as Seminole legend Jack Wingate calls them, will cover tree limbs that hang over the water and the bream fishing can be great.

Chad McClure and I were fishing with Mike Sloan, a guide and partner in Wingate's Lunker Lodge, targeting bream during the hatch in early June. Crows and a Green Heron were hopping from limb to limb eating the willow bugs, shaking the limbs and causing some of the mayflies to fall to the surface only to be gobbled up by slashing bream.

Chad was taking photos of the chaos with a long telephoto lens when he suddenly stopped shooting. "Y'all aren't gonna believe what this heron is doing," Chad said. Mike trolled the boat closer to the tree limbs as we watched something unbelievable transpire before our very eyes. This bird was delicately grabbing mayflies with the tip of his beak, hopping down to the lowest limb over the water and setting the fly on the surface. He would then stare intensely until a bream would rise to the fly, which would be the bream's last meal.

This should give us hope that if a bird brain can figure out how to fly fish Lake Seminole, we can too.

Anglers and herons alike know that Seminole is a great place to fish.

A mayfly hatch of Biblical proportions occurs on this lake in early June.

Flies to Use (continued)

#2-10 Gaines Sneaky Pete, #14-16 Black Ant Parachute, #8-12 Dave's Cricket, #6-10 Dave's Foam Hopper, #10-12 Yellow Jacket, #8-12 Damsel Parachute.

Sub-surface Flies: #1/0 Enrico's Bluegill, #1/0 Enrico's Shad, #4-10 Krystal Bugger, #4-10 Woolly Bugger, #4-6 Woolly Grubber, #4-10 Muddler Minnow, #4-8 White Beadhead Flash Zonker, #4-8 Zonker, #4-8 Conehead Double Bunny, #2/0-2 Clouser Minnow, #1 Cowen's Coyote, #6-8 Mickey Finn, #6 Matuka, #1/0-2 Lefty's Deceiver, #14-18 Black Ant, #1/0 Barr's Meat Whistle, #2-8 Chocklett's Gummy Minnow, #4-8 Whitlock's Near Nuff Crayfish, #4 Whitlock's Softshell Crayfish.

When to Fish

Mid-January through mid-May is awesome for targeting shallow largemouths, as are October and November. And a big mayfly hatch occurs in June that allows for sight-casting to bream and some bass.

Seasons & Limits

Seminole can be fished all year and falls under general sport fishing regulations. Part of the lake requires proper licensing from the state of Florida to be legally fished. Stay current on all of the regulations by visiting GoFishGeorgia.com.

Nearby Fly Fishing

The Flint River and the Chattahoochee River upstream of the lake provide good shoal bass fishing.

Accommodations & Services

If you're going to Seminole, you've got to stay at Wingate's Lunker Lodge near Bainbridge, Georgia. They have affordable and clean cabins with cold A/C, cable TV, mini-fridges, and a great restaurant with country cooking right on the water. It's also a good location for putting in a boat or getting picked up by a guide.

Helpful Web Sites

WingatesLodge.com
SloansReelSports.com
GON.com
GoFishGeorgia.com

Rating

Seminole is a dream for fly anglers who love the headshake of a truly big largemouth making it an easy 9 out of 10.

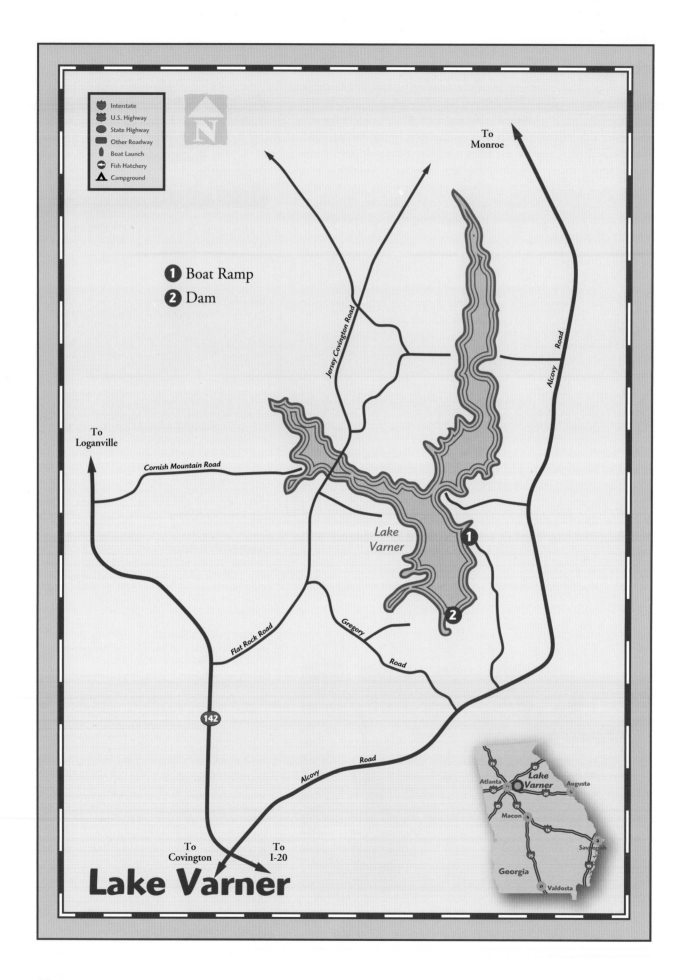

1 Boat Ramp
2 Dam

Interstate
U.S. Highway
State Highway
Other Roadway
Boat Launch
Fish Hatchery
Campground

To Monroe

Jersey Covington Road

Alcovy Road

To Loganville

Cornish Mountain Road

Lake Varner

Flat Rock Road

Gregory Road

142

Alcovy Road

To Covington

To I-20

Lake Varner

Georgia

Atlanta

Augusta

Macon

Savannah

Valdosta

Lake Varner

Lake Varner

More and more, fly anglers are broadening their angling horizons by straying from the usual quarries of trout and salmon. One exploding segment of the sport centers around the world's most popular game fish, the largemouth bass, and for good reason. While casting emergers to delicately sipping trout can be one of fly fishing's biggest challenges, sometimes the last thing an angler wants to feel is a subtle sip at the end of his tippet.

Luckily for the fly flinger with a wandering heart, large-mouths don't sip. They keep their pinkies down and use that more-displacement-than-a-V8-engine of a mouth to double-fist whatever has the bad fortune of being in their way. When it opens wide and sucks in you can almost see the lake level drop and hear subtlety go straight through the window.

Lake Varner is an 850-acre drinking water reservoir just east of Atlanta in Newton County that is, by all outward appearances, very unassuming. Even a die-hard bass fisherman unfamiliar with Varner might not give it a second glance if he drove by it. But, Varner is full of enough big mouths to make even the most proper dry fly fisherman yell, "Son!". The almost 16-pound lake record

Types of Fish
Largemouth bass, hybrid striped bass, bream, crappie, chain pickerel, and catfish.

Known Hatches
The most prevalent fish forage in Lake Varner is threadfin shad and gizzard shad. Golden shiners are also in the lake and the usual dragonflies and damselflies are abundant in warmer months.

Equipment to Use
Rods: 8-10 weight rods, 7 feet 11 inches to 9 feet in length (the heavier, the better as you'll need some backbone to pull these big fish out of the vegetation).

Reels: A reel with a good disc drag is needed for Varner's big fish.

Lines: Floating, intermediate, and sinking lines matched to rod weight.

Leaders: 7½-foot leaders tapered to 12-pound test for use with floating lines; 4'-6' leaders of straight 20-pound test for use with intermediate and sinking lines.

Wading: Walking the banks is an option when the bass are shallow in spring and fall. For the rest of the year a boat not employing the use of a gas-powered motor is needed.

An angler gets in a few more casts before sunset on Lake Varner. Photo by David Cannon

Bear Keeling fishes a rocky bank in search of a Varner lunker bass. Photo by David Cannon.

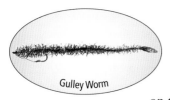
Gulley Worm

and multiple ten-plus-pound bass hooked here every year should have this lake packed seven days a week. But on weekdays, there are few boats on the water.

The lake formerly known as Cornish Creek Reservoir is a young one. It was constructed in 1991 and is still profiting from the soil nutrients from which young lakes benefit. In addition, cattle that continue to fertilize and add nutrients to this fishery utilize much of the land surrounding the lake, making it a sort of gigantic farm pond. And anyone who has ever spent time fishing a farm pond knows the big-bass potential.

Fly fishing for big Varner bass in the dead of winter usually means casting sinking lines and baitfish patterns over the main creek channels. This time of year, a rod with an intermediate line and something like a Clouser Minnow or Lefty's Deceiver should also be ready in case schooling hybrid striped bass push some threadfin or gizzard shad to the surface.

March is prime time for big bucketmouths and can be a sight caster's dream as big momma bass school in the shallows during the pre-spawn or when sizable shadows of expecting she-bass contrast against lighter beds below as the spawn ensues. Throwing floating lines and poppers, sliders, divers, and baitfish patterns for the remainder of spring can entice the shallow-lying bass until the dog days of summer drive them back to the creek channels.

And of course the cooling fall weather brings the fish shallow again, making it optimal for the fly angler. Then again, the optimal time to be chasing fish on Varner is anytime the opportunity arises.

Having a good selection of bass flies is a great idea on Lake Varner. Photo by David Cannon.

Flies to Use

Surface Flies: #4-6 DP Popper, #4-6 DP Slider, #10 Deer Hair Popper, #6 Dahlberg Diver, #2-6 Swimming Frog, #2 Deer Hair Mouse Rat, #1/0 Foammaster Frog, #2-10 Gaines Sneaky Pete, #14-16 Black Ant Parachute, #8-12 Dave's Cricket, #6-10 Dave's Foam Hopper, #10-12 Yellow Jacket, #8-12 Damsel Parachute.

Sub-surface Flies: #1/0 Enrico's Bluegill, #1/0 Enrico's Shad, #4-10 Krystal Bugger, #4-10 Woolly Bugger, #4-6 Woolly Grubber, #4-10 Muddler Minnow, #4-8 White Beadhead Flash Zonker, #4-8 Zonker, #4-8 Conehead Double Bunny, #2/0-2 Clouser Minnow, #1 Cowen's Coyote, #6-8 Mickey Finn, #6 Matuka, #1/0-2 Lefty's Deceiver, #14-18 Black Ant, #1/0 Barr's Meat Whistle, #2-8 Chocklett's Gummy Minnow, #1/0 to 3/0 Gulley Worm.

When to Fish

Because this lake gets no deeper than about 35 feet, fly anglers can pattern fish here all year. The best times are in spring and fall, when the bass are shallow.

Seasons & Limits

Open daily year-round from sunrise to sunset, Varner can be accessed via the park operated by Newton County. No gas motors allowed. Newton and Walton County residents can park and use the boat ramp for free, but nonresidents must pay a $5 parking fee and an additional $5 per boat. Bass must be at least 12 inches to be harvested, and the Georgia DNR recommends harvesting 12- to 18-inch bass and releasing bass more than 18 inches. View all of the regulations at GoFishGeorgia.com.

Nearby Fly Fishing

The Charlie Elliott Public Fishing Area is only about 15 miles southeast of Varner and has 22 fishing ponds.

Accommodations & Services

The city of Covington has plenty of lodgings and dining options. However, the closest dealer of fly gear is The Fish Hawk in the Buckhead area of Atlanta.

Rating

Big bass in a relatively shallow lake make for a great fly fisher's dream. I give it a solid 8 out of 10.

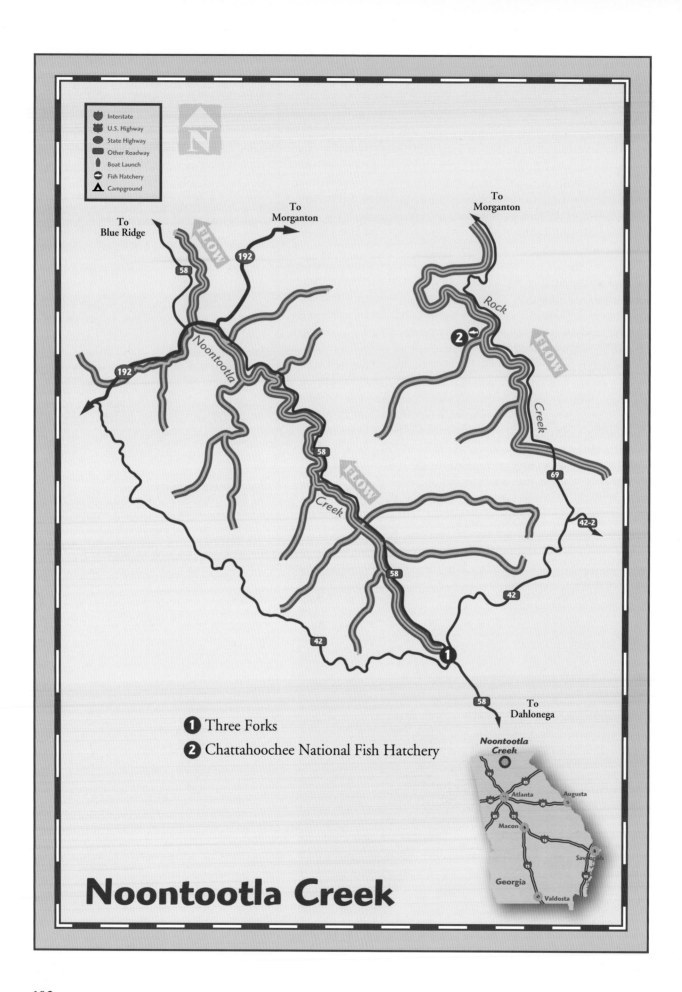

Legend:
- Interstate
- U.S. Highway
- State Highway
- Other Roadway
- Boat Launch
- Fish Hatchery
- Campground

To Blue Ridge

To Morganton

To Morganton

58

192

192

58

58

58

42

42

42-2

69

Noontootla

Creek

Rock

Creek

FLOW

FLOW

FLOW

1 Three Forks

2 Chattahoochee National Fish Hatchery

To Dahlonega

Noontootla Creek

Noontootla Creek

Georgia

Atlanta

Augusta

Macon

Savannah

Valdosta

Noontootla Creek

My schedule was completely open until dinnertime on my birthday one year and Noontootla Creek was on my short list of streams I really wanted to fish but hadn't yet. So, I hopped in the truck and headed to Blue Ridge, stopping in at Unicoi Outfitters for some advice and a few flies. Luckily for me, one of the friendliest and most knowledgeable guys in Georgia's fly fishing community, David Hulsey, was behind the counter that day and he was kind enough to offer his expertise.

Armed with David's advice and some proven fly patterns, I arrived and quickly got to work. I rigged the only fly rod I owned at the time—an all-too-long nine-footer I bought for $40—with a fresh 5X leader, a size 14 Light Cahill Parachute and a size 18 Adams Irresistible as a dropper. The first run I came to was too tight for fly casting, so I hid behind a rhododendron branch, choked up on the grip of my fly rod to shorten it and dapped my two dry flies onto the surface.

In a flash, a small wild rainbow grabbed the Irresistible and I quickly caught and released him. I set the flies down again on the

Types of Fish
Beautiful wild rainbows and browns. During a strong storm, a brook trout or two may get washed down from a feeder creek into Noontootla, too.

Known Hatches
Small Dun Caddis, Blue-Winged Olive, Blue Quill Mayfly, Midges, Winter Black Stonefly, Quill Gordon Mayfly, Light Cahill Mayfly, Early Black Stonefly, Cream Caddis, Red Quill/Hendrickson, March Brown Mayfly, Yellow Stonefly, Golden Stonefly, Speckled Grey Caddis, Giant Black Stonefly, Sulphur Mayfly, Green Drake Mayfly, Coffin Fly (Green Drake Spinner).

Equipment to Use
Rods: 3-4 weight, 7 to 8 feet in length.
Reels: Any reel that will hold your fly line will do.
Lines: Floating weight-forward or double-taper to match rod weight.
Leaders: 5X to 6X, 9 feet in length.
Wading: Chest waders are the best option for navigating some of the deeper stretches and wet-wading is great in the summer.

Flies to Use
See the Southern Appalachian Freestone Hatch Chart to correctly match the hatch.

Dry Flies: #14-16 Black Ant Parachute, #12 Dave's Cricket, #6-10 Dave's Foam Hopper, #10-12 Yellow Jacket, #14-20 Adams, #14-20 Adams Parachute,

Continued

Carter Morris navigates tight casting quarters on Noontootla.

*Carter Morris high sticks a fishy run on one of
Georgia's best trout streams, Noontootla Creek.*

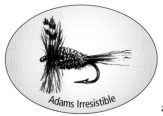
Adams Irresistible

same seam and another fish rose a foot behind the spot where the rainbow hit. I pulled this tiny creature to me and was shocked to see the unmistakable worm-like markings of a brook trout, a fish that must have been washed down from a feeder creek by the storm waters of a hurricane that had hit only a week before. This was already shaping up to be a pretty good birthday.

After slipping that little guy back into the cool water, I reached my rod some seven feet to the other side of the creek and dapped my flies again. After a few drifts, a large fish came out of the shadows and slashed at the Cahill. I was caught completely off guard, which usually results in either a premature strike or a late one. Somehow, I was caught in the middle of both reactions and Lady Luck helped me to set the hook at just the right time.

I immediately pulled the fish onto the bank and, at first, had no idea what I was holding. This strange trout had the fins of a brook trout—black with a heavy brushstroke of white on the edges. But its entire body was neon orange and adorned with only about eight spots on either side, half of which were black and the other half that same neon orange.

As my pulse started its descent out of the danger zone, some rationale returned and I identified this amazing trout as a brown. And while I didn't have a tape measure on me, I was able to estimate its length at 16 inches—a measurement I was pretty familiar with from framing walls during my summers in high school.

I quickly understood why Noontootla is closely guarded. Like other streams in Georgia that can support naturally reproducing trout, this location is fairly hush-hush. It's small, but not too small, tumbles through a lush and picturesque valley and is teeming with gorgeous fish. And while I learned on subsequent trips that this creek isn't usually so giving, over the next three hours that day I was able to land another 14 trout. Perhaps the best part was that I didn't have to switch flies once. If only every day was a birthday!

Noontootla trout have plenty to eat thanks to healthy populations of aquatic insects and big meals like this stonefly.

Flies to Use (continued)

#16-18 Adams Irresistible, #16-20 Blue Quill, #16-20 BWO, #18-22 Griffith's Gnat, #16-20 Elk Hair Caddis, #12-14 Quill Gordon, #14-16 Red Quill, #14-16 Hendrickson, #14 March Brown, #14 March Brown Parachute, #14-16 Yellow Stimulator, #12-18 Light Cahill, #12-18 Light Cahill Parachute, #14-18 Sulphur Comparadun, #14-18 Cream Variant, #12-14 Blue Dun Parachute, #8-10 Green Drake, #8-10 Spent-wing Coffin Fly, #8-10 Parachute Coffin Fly, #20-22 Parachute Trico, #20-22 Black Poly Wing Spinner.

Nymphs: #14-16 San Juan Worm, #14-20 Prince Nymph, #14-20 Hare's Ear Nymph, #14-16 Zug Bug, #14-20 Pheasant Tail, #16-20 Lightning Bug, #16-20 Rainbow Warrior, #18-22 Zebra Midge, #18-22 Disco Midge, #18-22 WD-40, #18-22 Midge Pupa, #16-20 Black Stonefly Nymph, #14-16 Yellow Stonefly Nymph, #4-8 Golden Stonefly Nymph, #4-8 Black Stonefly Nymph, #12-14 Quill Gordon Nymph, #12-14 Light Cahill Nymph, #8-10 Green Drake Nymph.

Streamers: #10-14 Krystal Bugger, #10-14 Woolly Bugger, #10-14 Muddler Minnow, #8 White Beadhead Flash Zonker, #8 Zonker, #10 Mickey Finn, #10 Black-nosed Dace.

When to Fish

Noontootla is an amazing stream that can be fished all year long. If you get an opportunity to go, even if it's in the heat of the summer or the dead of winter, just do it.

Seasons & Limits

Noontootla can be fished year-round with artificial lures only. Only fish in excess of 16 inches can be harvested and catch and release is encouraged.

Nearby Fly Fishing

Noontootla's feeder creeks can be phenomenal, but don't tell anyone you read that here. Travel upstream and over the mountain to reach wild brown trout stream, Jones Creek, or head back towards Blue Ridge to fish the upper Toccoa, the Toccoa delayed harvest section, the Toccoa tailwater downstream (north) of Blue Ridge Reservoir, or the lake for smallmouth bass. If you'd like to treat yourself, book a trip at Noontootla Creek Farms, which is trophy managed and full of big, beautiful trout.

Accommodations & Services

Unicoi Outfitters in Blue Ridge is the closest fly shop to Noontootla and it can be a great idea to hire a guide from there for your first trip to this challenging stream. There are cabins for rent in the Aska Adventure area between Noontootla and the town of Blue Ridge, which also has plenty of lodging and dining spots.

Helpful Web Sites

UnicoiOutfitters.com
GoFishGeorgia.com

Rating

Noontootla can be very challenging, and it arguably holds the most beautiful wild trout in the Southeast. Beautiful fish in a beautiful Southern Appalachian high-gradient stream makes for a 10 out of 10.

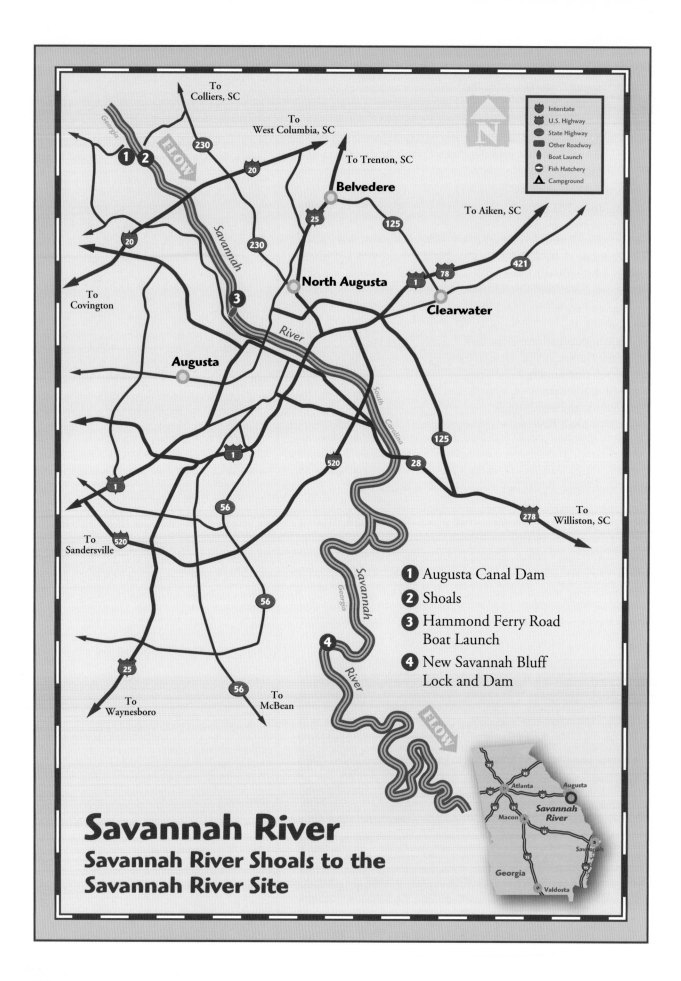

Savannah River
Savannah River Shoals to the
Savannah River Site

Legend:
- Interstate
- U.S. Highway
- State Highway
- Other Roadway
- Boat Launch
- Fish Hatchery
- Campground

To Colliers, SC
To West Columbia, SC
To Trenton, SC
Belvedere
To Aiken, SC
To Covington
North Augusta
Clearwater
Augusta
To Sandersville
To Williston, SC
To Waynesboro
To McBean

1 Augusta Canal Dam
2 Shoals
3 Hammond Ferry Road Boat Launch
4 New Savannah Bluff Lock and Dam

Georgia
Savannah River
South Carolina

Atlanta
Augusta
Macon
Savannah
Georgia
Valdosta

Savannah River

Savannah River Shoals to the Savannah River Site

A popping bug is often enough to entice multiple species that inhabit the Savannah River.

It's funny, but if I'm not careful I can find myself feeling legitimately sorry for someone who doesn't fly fish, as if not enjoying it equates to some sort of actual affliction. "I've never fly fished before," sounds almost as sad to me as someone saying, "I just found out I have the plague." Almost as bad, though, are fly anglers who only fish for one species. Don't get me wrong, I love fishing for trout. But if you can catch any species that swims on a fly, many of which are naturally larger than browns or rainbows, why not do it?

For a smorgasbord of angling variety, the Savannah River offers the chance at a multitude of species. And more specifically, the stretch surrounding the town of Augusta—from the Savannah River Shoals where the Augusta Canal originates down past the New Savannah Bluff Lock and Dam and to a point just upstream of the Savannah River Site—is a great one to explore and a great way to give a few of your fly rods a workout in the same day.

American shad start showing up in this area as early as February and hang around through the spring. These fish run from the

Russ Lumpkin, managing editor of Gray's Sporting Journal, American Angler, *and* Fly Tyer *magazines, casts around a cypress tree for river bass.*

Russ Lumpkin enjoying a productive day on the Savannah.

Clouser Minnow

Atlantic and are stalled at the Lock and Dam until opened to allow for their continued travel upriver. These fish are a blast on a five-weight rod and tend to favor sparsely-tied baitfish patterns like Clouser Minnows.

On the tail fins of the shad, however, runs the main attraction—big stripers. In the early spring and going into mid-summer, stripers follow mullet running up the river. While most of these fish stay in the "Striper Alley" area—a run of four to five miles below the New Lock and Dam—some do sneak up the lock with the shad. Smaller fish will be caught, but the bulk of the linesides you'll see are in the 15- to 50-pound range, calling for 10-weight rods rigged with fast-sinking lines, a 30-pound test leader and mullet patterns as long as 10 inches. These fish are generally found in slack water near strong current or on sand or gravel bars from early spring through mid-summer.

Above and below the New Lock and Dam, largemouth, spotted, and redeye bass can be targeted with standard bass flies. Shellcrackers of potentially gigantic proportions are caught out of this river every year. We're talking panfish that sometimes reach weights of more than three pounds!

What I'm about to tell you is still largely unknown in angling circles and probably involves the illegal placement of fish into habitat, which is never a good idea. However, a "bucket biologist" likely took the liberty of introducing smallmouth bass to the Savannah River upstream of the New Lock and Dam. It's been argued for years that the fish would do extremely well in this stretch of the river because of its rocky habitat and cool waters. And although the Georgia DNR always insisted that the introduction of smallies to this river would decimate the native redeye bass population, someone dumped them in anyway. While this behavior is illegal and should not be condoned, the fact of the matter is smallmouth bass are now in the river and are doing well. So, we might as well welcome them by tossing a fly their way.

Smallmouth bass started showing up in the river in 2007 and are now a popular target for anglers.

Types of Fish

For fly anglers, the focus can be on big stripers, redeye, largemouth, and spotted bass, huge shellcrackers and, the latest to be (illegally) introduced to the river, the ferocious smallmouth bass. A run of American Shad is noteworthy, as well.

Known Hatches

The mullet "hatch" (or run) is the key one for striper anglers. Other fish forage consists mainly of baitfish.

Equipment to Use

Rods: 5-10 weight, 7 feet 11 inches to 10 feet in length.
Reels: Standard disc drag. A large-arbor reel is a good choice here.
Lines: Floating weight-forward to match rod weight, intermediate lines, 350-450 grain sinking lines.
Leaders: 7- to 9-foot leaders for floating lines, 4- to 6-foot leaders of 20- or 30-pound test for sinking lines when striper fishing.
Wading: This is big water and a boat is a big asset here. Floating a canoe or kayak can gain you access to wadeable shoal areas.

Flies to Use

Surface Flies: #4-2/0 Blados's Crease Fly, #1/0-2/0 pencil popper, #6-4 DP Popper, #6-4 DP Slider, #4-2 Sneaky Pete.

Subsurface Flies: #4-2 Cowen's Somethin' Else, #1/0 Cowen's Baitfish, #4/0 Cowen's Magnum Baitfish, #1 Cowen's Coyote, #2/0-2 Clouser Minnow, #2-8 Chocklett's Gummy Minnow, #2/0-4 Lefty's Deceiver, #4-2 Mayfield's Rattle Mullet, #2-1/0 Cowen's Mullet, #2/0 Puglisi Mullet, #3/0 Kintz' Major Mullet.

When to Fish

Plenty of fish can be caught here all year, but focus on late winter to early spring for American Shad, early spring to mid-summer for stripers, and August through October for panfish and bass.

Seasons & Limits

The Savannah River is a year-round fishery that can be legally fished with either proper licensing from either the state of Georgia or South Carolina through a reciprocal agreement. See GoFishGeorgia.com for a complete rundown of regulations.

Nearby Fly Fishing

Clarks Hill Reservoir is a great place to chase hybrids, stripers, and largemouth bass on the fly, and Brier Creek, which is a tributary of the Savannah and has a historic run of red-bellies.

Accommodations & Services

Rivers & Glen Trading Company, a fly shop in Augusta, is fully stocked with flies and tackle. A Bass Pro Shops is also in the works in the Augusta area.

Helpful Web Sites

RiversandGlen.com
GeorgiaRiverFishing.com

Rating

The variety alone makes this river a 9 out of 10.

Edge of the Hole by Bucky Bowles.

Bucky Bowles.
©2004

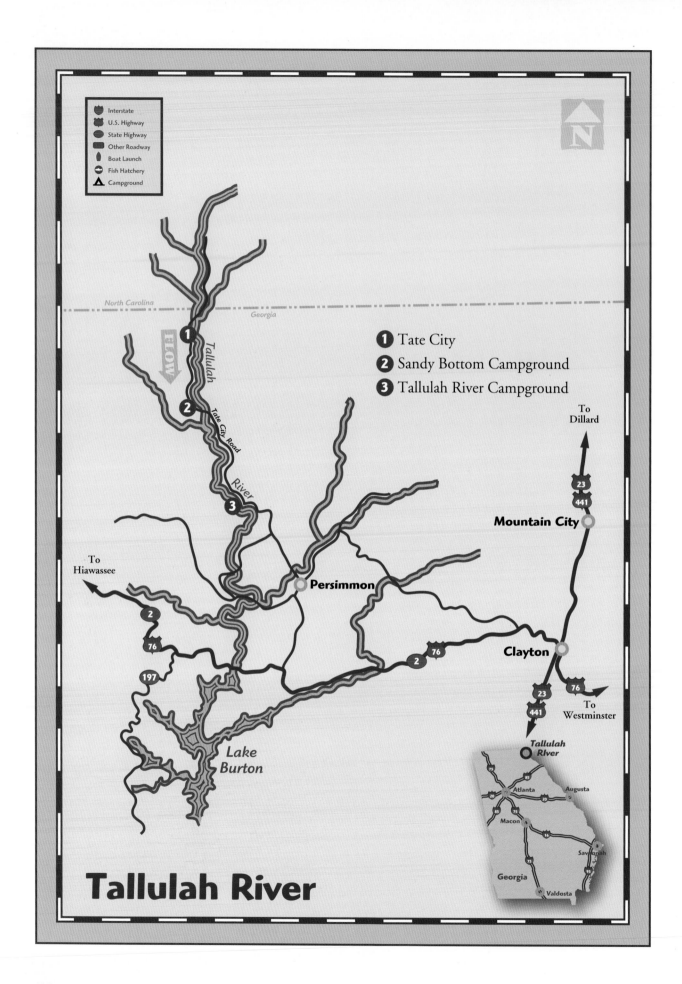

Legend
- Interstate
- U.S. Highway
- State Highway
- Other Roadway
- Boat Launch
- Fish Hatchery
- Campground

North Carolina

Georgia

Tallulah

Tate City Road

River

1 Tate City
2 Sandy Bottom Campground
3 Tallulah River Campground

To
Dillard

23
441

Mountain City

To
Hiawassee

2

76

197

2   76

Clayton

23
441

76
To
Westminster

Persimmon

Lake
Burton

Tallulah River

Tallulah River

Atlanta   Augusta

Macon

Savannah

Georgia

Valdosta

Tallulah River

egend has it that the daughter of Cherokee Indian Chief Grey Eagle found a lost white man wandering the Cherokee trail and brought him back to her camp. The natives viewed the presence of a white in their camp as bad luck, so Grey Eagle sentenced him to death. As the story goes, the princess grew fond of the foreigner and threatened to jump off of the cliff into the river, the same one he would be thrown off of after being tied up. Her threats went unheard and, when her lover met his fate, she followed and threw herself into the violent waters rushing through the gorge below.

The cliff this princess of legend leapt off of is now known as "Lover's Leap" and the river in which she met her fabled end now bares her name—Tallulah.

Miles upstream of the gorge, the Tallulah is a smaller, more peaceful setting. Its high origin on Standing Indian Mountain in North Carolina does make this small stream flow quite violently, as drastic elevation drops continue across its first few miles into Georgia and through Rabun County. Though only 10- to

Types of Fish
Rainbow and brown trout.

Known Hatches
Small Dun Caddis, Blue-Winged Olive, Blue Quill Mayfly, Midges, Winter Black Stonefly, Quill Gordon Mayfly, Light Cahill Mayfly, Early Black Stonefly, Cream Caddis, Red Quill/Hendrickson, March Brown Mayfly, Yellow Stonefly, Golden Stonefly, Speckled Grey Caddis, Giant Black Stonefly, Sulphur Mayfly, Green Drake Mayfly, Coffin Fly (Green Drake Spinner).

Equipment to Use
Rods: 3-5 weight, 7½ to 8½ feet in length.
Reels: Any mechanical fly reel.
Lines: Floating weight-forward or double-taper to match rod weight.
Leaders: 4X-6X leaders, 9 feet in length.
Wading: There are some deep holes in the Tallulah, warranting the use of chest waders.

A Tallulah River rainbow goes airborne after being hooked.

David Cannon works one of many deep runs on the Tallulah.

Hare's Ear Nymph

15-feet wide in the upper stretch in our northeastern-most county, the Tallulah bores its way through gigantic boulders, rounds ancient bedrock, and creates some deceptively deep holes.

While all of this creates some potentially treacherous wading, it also affords some wonderful holds for the trout of the river. And, if present at the right time, you'll find this river can have a lot of fish swimming its waters.

The Tallulah is what is commonly known as a "put-and-take" fishery, or one that is stocked heavily and has its fish harvested rapidly by those wanting an accompaniment to their hush puppies and slaw. However, there are wild fish in this river and catching one of them amongst the stockers is a real treat. These wild fish, though small, are wonderfully colored and strike fast enough to test the quickest of reflexes.

Just downstream of Tate City, a community of only a couple hundred people, there is a great potential for hooking into a big rainbow. Some of the residents here add supplemental feed to the water and the fish within the safe boundaries of the private property grow big and strong as a result. Occasionally a brute will wander down into public water and surprise a visiting angler. So, be ready for anything when fishing this area.

While this river should be avoided like the plague between Memorial and Labor Days, fly anglers should utilize three campsites along the upper river in the winter months when the camping crowds thin. These sites can serve as a great base for a long weekend's worth of angling exploration either in the Tallulah or one of its great tributaries. The wild fish of these streams offer some diversity when contrasted against fishing for the many stocked trout of the Tallulah. Take a kid or a friend wanting to learn the sport and leap into the Tallulah—just not from the top of the gorge.

Flashy flies work well for the many stocked trout on this river, while more natural offerings can tempt the wild trout that inhabit its waters.

Flies to Use

See the Southern Appalachian Freestone Hatch Chart to correctly match the hatch.

Dry Flies: #8-20 Adams, #8-20 Adams Parachute, #16-20 BWO, #16-22 Griffith's Gnat, #14-20 Elk Hair Caddis, #14-16 Yellow Stimulator, #12-16 Royal Wulff, #12-16 Yellow Humpy, #12-18 Light Cahill, #12-18 Light Cahill Parachute, #14-18 Sulphur Comparadun, #14-16 Dark Elk Hair Caddis with Green, #14-16 Dark Elk Hair Caddis with Yellow and Brown, #20-22 Parachute Trico, #20-22 Black Poly Wing Spinner, #8-10 Ginger Elk Hair Caddis.

Nymphs & Wet Flies: #14-16 Y2K Bug, #14-16 Glo Egg, #14-16 San Juan Worm, #12-20 Prince Nymph, #12-20 Hare's Ear Nymph, #12-16 Zug Bug, #8-20 Pheasant Tail, #16-18 Caddis Pupa, #18-22 Midge Pupa, #16-20 Black Stonefly Nymph, #14-16 Yellow Stonefly Nymph, #4-8 Golden Stonefly Nymph, #4-8 Black Stonefly Nymph, #18-20 Lightning Bug, #18-20 Rainbow Warrior.

Streamers: #6-12 Krystal Bugger, #6-12 Woolly Bugger, #6-12 Muddler Minnow, #4-8 White Beadhead Flash Zonker, #4-8 Zonker, #6-10 Mickey Finn, #6-10 Black-nosed Dace.

When to Fish

Winter fishing here can be very good, especially because the camping crowds have thinned.

Seasons & Limits

The Tallulah is open for fishing 12 months of the year. However, all of its tributaries except for Charles Creek are seasonal. Also, portions of the Coleman River—another feeder stream of the Tallulah—fall under artificials-only regulations.

Nearby Fly Fishing

The Tallulah's tributaries are fun to explore. And either fork of the Chattooga and its tributaries offer good fly fishing. Sixty percent of Rabun County is public land, so opportunities abound.

Accommodations & Services

The Reeves Ace Hardware store in Clayton has a good fly selection and necessary fly tackle.

Helpful Web Sites

RabunTU.com
NGTO.org
GoFishGeorgia.com

Rating

This put-and-take fishery is a scenic one and is wonderful for taking kids or anyone new to fly fishing. I rate it a 6 out of 10.

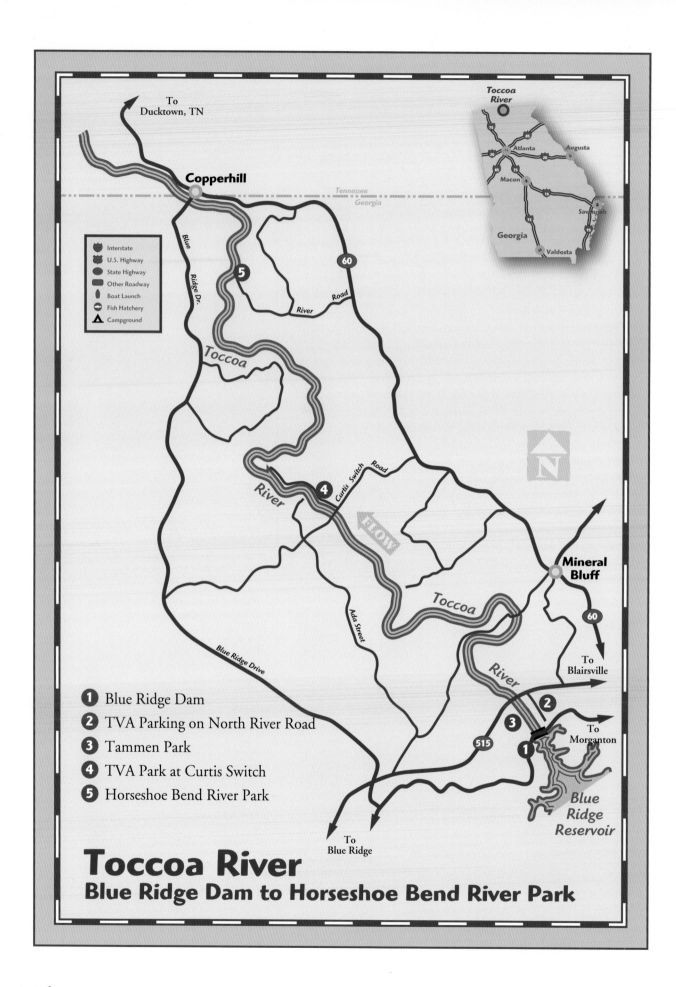

To
Ducktown, TN

Toccoa
River

Copperhill

Tennessee
Georgia

Interstate
U.S. Highway
State Highway
Other Roadway
Boat Launch
Fish Hatchery
Campground

Blue
Ridge Dr.

Toccoa

River

Road

River

60

5

Atlanta
Augusta
Macon
Savannah
Georgia
Valdosta

N

Curtis Switch Road

4

FLOW

Ada Street

Toccoa

**Mineral
Bluff**

60

To
Blairsville

Blue Ridge Drive

River

To
Morganton

1 Blue Ridge Dam
2 TVA Parking on North River Road
3 Tammen Park
4 TVA Park at Curtis Switch
5 Horseshoe Bend River Park

2

3

515

1

**Blue
Ridge
Reservoir**

To
Blue Ridge

Toccoa River
Blue Ridge Dam to Horseshoe Bend River Park

Toccoa River

Blue Ridge Dam to Curtis Switch

A book focusing on the state of Georgia may not be the place for this statement, but I'm originally from Texas. I'm admitting this because I have a slightly different perspective when something is described as big. "Big" reminds me of Big Tex at the state fair, the unending Texas sky, and even my own mother's big Texas hairdo and big personality.

When my dad's job moved us out of the Lone Star State, we were able to settle in the biggest state east of the Mississippi. And, true to its size, Georgia has some claims to "big," as well. I now think of the Georgia Aquarium, Stone Mountain, and, of course, the Big Chicken. When it comes to trout fishing in Georgia, it doesn't get much bigger than the Toccoa River tailwater.

There are roughly 16 miles of tailwater running south to north from Blue Ridge Dam to the Tennessee state line where the Toccoa's name changes to Ocoee. And within that length, the river is generally broken into two sections. The first, which we will cover in this chapter, is the approximately 7.2 miles of water from the dam down to the Tennessee Valley Authority (TVA) park at Curtis Switch.

On a side note, 7.2 miles of river might not sound like a tough stretch to float over the course of a day. But even during the longer

Types of Fish
Rainbow, brown, and brook trout, and the occasional smallmouth, largemouth, spotted or rock bass, yellow perch, and bream.

Known Hatches
Midges, Black Stonefly, Black Caddis, Gray Midges, Gray Caddis, Quill Gordon, Blue Dun, Blue-Winged Olive, March Brown, Hendrickson, Olive Caddis, Sulphurs, Little Yellow Stonefly, Green Drake, Light Cahill, Tan Caddis, Yellow Drake, October Caddis, Terrestrials.

Equipment to Use
Rods: 4-5 weights for nymphs and dry flies, 6-7 weights for streamers. Both should be 8½ to 10 feet long.

Reels: It's a good idea to use a reel with a disc drag in case you run into one of the larger fish here.

Lines: Floating lines to match rod weight when fishing dries or nymphs, intermediate lines to match rod weight when fishing streamers.

Leaders: 9- to 12-foot leaders tapered from 4-6X when fishing floating lines, 5- to 7-foot leaders tapered from 1-3X when fishing intermediate lines.

Wading: Floating in anything but a float tube is the best way to experience this fishery and chest waders are the best choice when hopping out of your watercraft to fish.

Flies to Use
See the Toccoa River Tailwater Hatch Chart to correctly match the hatch.

Dry Flies: #22-28 Morgan's Para Midge, #18 Lowe's Little Dark Stonefly, #16-18 Black Elk Hair Caddis,

Continued

Fishing foggy summer evenings on the Toccoa can prove to be very productive.

Toccoa River Tailwater Hatch Chart

Compiled by David Hulsey and courtesy of Unicoi Outfitters

Insect	Jan	Feb	Mar	April	May	June	July	Aug	Sept	Oct	Nov	Dec
Midges	■	■								■	■	■
Black Stonefly	■	■									■	■
Black Caddis	■	■										
Gray Midges		■	■									
Gray Caddis			■									
Quill Gordon			■									
Blue Dun			■									
Blue-Winged Olive										■	■	■
March Brown				■								
Hendrickson				■								
Olive Caddis				■								
Sulphurs					■	■						
Little Yellow Stonefly					■							
Green Drake					■							
Light Cahill						■	■	■	■			
Tan Caddis						■	■	■	■			
Yellow Drake							■	■				
Terrestrials							■	■	■			
October Caddis										■		

Insect	Sizes	Dry Flies	Nymphs
Midges	22-26	Morgan's Para Midge	Midge Pupa, Brassie, Serendipity, WD-40
Black Stonefly	18	Lowe's Little Dark Stonefly	Black Stonefly Nymph
Black Caddis	16-18	Black Elk Hair Caddis	Black Caddis Pupa, Pheasant Tail Nymph
Gray Midges	22-28	Morgan's Para Midge	Midge Pupa, Brassie, Serendipity, WD-40
Gray Caddis	16-18	Gray Elk Hair Caddis	Dun and Yellow Caddis Pupa
Quill Gordon	14	Quill Gordon	Quill Gordon Nymph
Blue Dun	16	Blue Dun	Blue Dun Nymph, Pheasant Tail Nymph
Blue-Winged Olive	22-24	Parachute BWO	BWO Nymph, Pheasant Tail Nymph
March Brown	14	Eastern March Brown	March Brown Nymph, Dark Hare's Ear Nymph, Pheasant Tail Nymph
Hendrickson	14-16	Dark Hendrickson	Dark Hendrickson Nymph, Pheasant Tail Nymph
Olive Caddis	16	Olive Elk Hair Caddis	Dun and Green Caddis Pupa, Olive Hare's Ear Nymph
Sulphurs	16-18	Sulphur Comparadun	Sulphur Nymph, Pheasant Tail Nymph
Little Yellow Stonefly	16	North Carolina Yellow Sally	Yellow Stonefly Nymph
Green Drake	10	Coffin Fly	Green Drake Nymph
Light Cahill	14	Parachute Light Cahill	Light Cahill Nymph, Hare's Ear Nymph
Tan Caddis	16-18	Tan Elk Hair Caddis	Tan Caddis Pupa, Hare's Ear Nymph
Yellow Drake	12	Jim Charlie Classic	Yellow Drake Nymph, Hare's Ear Nymph
Terrestrials	Various	Black Ant, Foam Beetle, Dave's Hopper	Hardbody Ant, Woolly Worm
October Caddis	12	Elk Hair October Caddis	Ginger Caddis Pupa, Pheasant Tail Nymph

Sulphur Comparadun

daylight hours of summer, many shallow shoal areas slow down even the highest floating watercraft. This float can be done in a day, but time spent working the best water will be too short if you want to make it to Curtis Switch before it gets dark. And believe me, you do. A good alternative is renting a cabin somewhere between these access points and floating either from the dam to the cabin or from the cabin down to Curtis Switch. Toccoa House Properties has four nice cabins almost exactly halfway between the points.

As you float farther away from the access points, the fishing only gets better. Plenty of rainbows and browns 20 inches or more are caught every year and are almost always landed away from a public put-in. Of course, a few big browns might be hanging around the dam or Curtis Switch, too, just waiting for their snack truck to dump in a few thousand smaller rainbow trout. With this in mind, don't neglect a proven tactic on the tailwater—casting a 6- or 7-weight rod with an intermediate line and a big streamer to entice those carnivorous browns.

Of course, if fishing dry flies is your thing, this section can offer that all year long. During the summer months, the cold water of the Toccoa meets the sweltering summer air and, in shaded areas, creates a nice layer of fog. This probably makes the fish lose some of their inhibitions and definitely helps to keep anglers out of sight—a pretty good combination.

If you enjoy fishing streamers and dry flies, the worst thing about the Toccoa is the dilemma it presents—do you tie on a fly that imitates the insects or one that looks like a stocker rainbow? Maybe you should take two rods.

Legendary Georgia author and editor Jimmy Jacobs casts to a rising brown in glassy water.

Flies to Use (continued)

#16-18 Gray Elk Hair Caddis, #14 Quill Gordon, #16 Blue Dun, #22-24 Parachute BWO, #14 Eastern March Brown, #14-16 Dark Hendrickson, #16 Olive Elk Hair Caddis, #16-18 Sulphur Comparadun, #16 North Carolina Yellow Sally, #10 Coffin Fly, #14 Parachute Light Cahill, #16-18 Tan Elk Hair Caddis, #12 Jim Charlie Classic, #12 Elk Hair October Caddis, #14-18 Black Ant, #10-12 Foam Beetle, #8-12 Dave's Hopper, #14-18 Adams Parachute, #12-16 Stimulator, #14-18 Adams Irresistible

Nymphs: #22-28 Midge Pupa, #22-28 Brassie, #22-28 Serendipity, #22-28 WD-40, #18 Black Stonefly Nymph, #16-18 Black Caddis Pupa, #12-22 Pheasant Tail Nymph, #16-18 Dun and Yellow Caddis Pupa, #14 Quill Gordon Nymph, #16 Blue Dun Nymph, #22-24 BWO Nymph, #14 March Brown Nymph, #14 Dark Hare's Ear Nymph, #14-16 Dark Hendrickson Nymph, #16 Dun and Green Caddis Pupa, #16 Olive Hare's Ear Nymph, #16-18 Sulphur Nymph, #16 Yellow Stonefly Nymph, #10 Green Drake Nymph, #14 Light Cahill Nymph, #14-18 Hare's Ear Nymph, #12 Yellow Drake Nymph, #12 Ginger Caddis Pupa, #14-16 Hardbody Ant, #8-12 Woolly Worm, #16-20 Lightning Bug, #16-20 Rainbow Warrior, #14 San Juan Worm, #14 Y2K Bug, #10 Hurless Nymph.

Streamers: #6-10 Krystal Bugger, #6-10 Woolly Bugger, #6-10 Muddler Minnow, #8 White Beadhead Flash Zonker, #8 Zonker, #6-10 Mickey Finn, #6-10 Black-nosed Dace.

When to Fish

The only time fishing slows is when Blue Ridge Reservoir turns over. Other than those times, fish here every chance you get, particularly when the water is falling after the generator at the dam turns off.

Seasons & Limits

The Toccoa tailwater is open to fishing all year and is under general regulations.

Nearby Fly Fishing

Jones Creek, Noontootla Creek, trophy-managed Noontootla Creek Farms, the upper Toccoa including the Toccoa delayed harvest, Blue Ridge Reservoir, and plenty of other small streams are all within a short drive of this section of the tailwater.

Accommodations & Services

Toccoa House Properties offers four different well-appointed cabins roughly halfway between the dam and Curtis Switch—the perfect location for splitting this long float in half. Unicoi Outfitters, Reel Job Fishing, Reel Angling Adventures, Southeastern Anglers, and Feather & Fly all guide on this river. The only fly shop in the area, however, is Unicoi Outfitters in downtown Blue Ridge.

Helpful Information

FeatherandFly.com, GoFishGeorgia.com
Kent-Klewein.com, NGTO.org
ReelAnglingAdventures.com
SoutheasternAnglers.com
ToccoaHouse.com
UnicoiOutfitters.com

TVA (Water Release Information): (800) 238-2264

Rating

This section of the Toccoa is great all year long and deserves nothing less than a 9 out of 10.

Drift boats are a popular way of navigating the Toccoa tailwater.

Toccoa River

Curtis Switch to Horseshoe Bend River Park

As if the first seven plus miles of this great river weren't enough, there are another six miles of very good water below Curtis Switch just waiting to be fished. The six-mile journey downstream, or north in the case of the Toccoa, to Horseshoe Bend River Park in McCaysville offers a wider, mostly shallower continuation of the great trout water that flows from the depths of Blue Ridge Reservoir.

Guide David Hulsey tells a story about this section. "We were on a morning guide trip at Horseshoe Bend River Park one foggy May morning. We slid in the water early and started working upstream casting sulfur mayflies to eager trout. For about an hour it was a fly fisher's dream, catching and releasing beautiful rainbow after rainbow. A ragged sulphur comparadun caused a temporary pause in the action. As I shuffled through my fly box a sudden explosion of water just upstream almost made us jump out of our waders! Out of this eruption of river water, a huge wake took off at warp speed straight toward the sandy riverbank.

Types of Fish

Rainbow, brown, and brook trout are the primary targets and you may stumble on the occasional smallmouth, largemouth, spotted or rock bass, yellow perch, or bream.

Known Hatches

Midges, Black Stonefly, Black Caddis, Gray Midges, Gray Caddis, Quill Gordon, Blue Dun, Blue-Winged Olive, March Brown, Hendrickson, Olive Caddis, Sulphurs, Little Yellow Stonefly, Green Drake, Light Cahill, Tan Caddis, Yellow Drake, October Caddis, Terrestrials.

Equipment to Use

Rods: 4-5 weights for nymphs and dry flies, 6-7 weights for streamers. Both should be 8½ to 10 feet long.

Reels: It's a good idea to use a reel with a disc drag in case you run into one of the larger fish here.

Lines: Floating lines to match rod weight when fishing dries or nymphs, intermediate lines to match rod weight when fishing streamers.

Leaders: 9- to 12-foot leaders tapered from 4-6X when fishing floating lines, 5- to 7-foot leaders tapered from 1-3X when fishing intermediate lines.

Wading: This is pretty big water by Georgia trout fishing standards, so chest waders are the best choice.

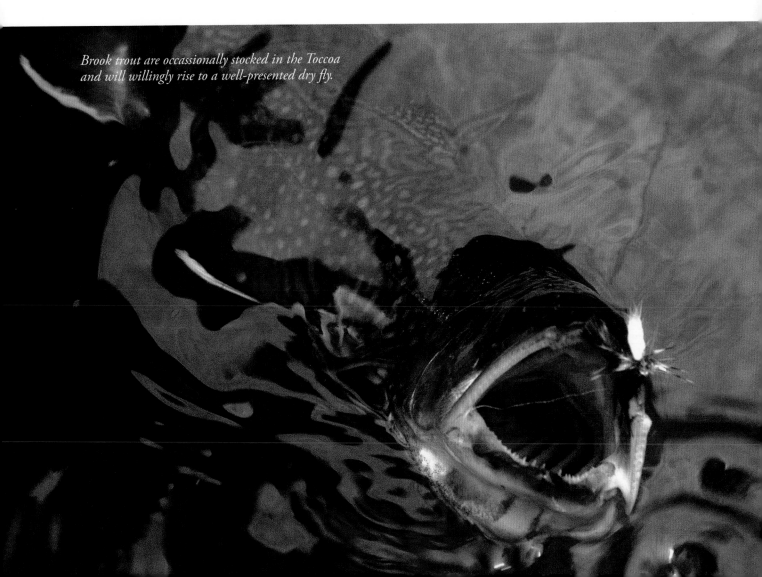

Brook trout are occasionally stocked in the Toccoa and will willingly rise to a well-presented dry fly.

Two anglers fight fish as they drift past Curtis Switch.

Beadhead Flash Zonker

Expecting to see an otter or beaver crawl out onto the shore we were surprised to see a 12-inch rainbow clear the water and land some 4-feet up in the grass. A millisecond later a huge brown trout almost beached himself trying to hit the brakes! After a few hops around on the bank the unlucky rainbow bounced back to the waters edge and plopped into the river into the mouth of the waiting monster. My client turned to me slack jawed and mumbled, 'What was that?' Needless to say we threw streamers the rest of the morning!"

The closer you get to Horseshoe Bend River Park, the fewer fish you are going to come across. But, even at the park, as David and his client experienced, the numbers are still good. The fewer numbers of fish can probably be attributed to the warming temperatures in the hot summer months. Populations of caddis, mayflies, and midges are all still strong throughout this run. This, coupled with the regular stockings of fingerling and catchable sized rainbow and brown trout, allows for the growth of some trophy fish. And, the lower section of the Toccoa doesn't see quite the float traffic the upper section does, which can really play to the angler's favor.

A good option in the warmer months is drifting from Curtis Switch to a point about three to four miles downstream. Finding yourself in the middle of the sulphur hatch in May or June or a light cahill or caddis hatch in June through September can be an exciting experience. The lawns and pastures on both sides of the Toccoa also contribute grasshoppers and ants with a little help from a stiff breeze. Tiny blue-winged olives can hatch sporadically in the hot weather and potentially tinier midges present a real challenge to dry-fly aficionados any time of the year.

A word to the wise—floating any stretch of the Toccoa in a float tube is a bad idea. But, floating this portion of it is a particularly bad plan because of its increase in wide shallow areas. In a float tube you'll likely end up walking with it more than you'll float it.

A hefty Toccoa River brown trout. Photo by David Cannon.

Flies to Use

See the Toccoa River Tailwater Hatch Chart to correctly match the hatch.

Dry Flies: #22-28 Morgan's Para Midge, #18 Lowe's Little Dark Stonefly, #16-18 Black Elk Hair Caddis, #16-18 Gray Elk Hair Caddis, #14 Quill Gordon, #16 Blue Dun, #22-24 Parachute BWO, #14 Eastern March Brown, #14-16 Dark Hendrickson, #16 Olive Elk Hair Caddis, #16-18 Sulphur Comparadun, #16 North Carolina Yellow Sally, #10 Coffin Fly, #14 Parachute Light Cahill, #16-18 Tan Elk Hair Caddis, #12 Jim Charlie Classic, #12 Elk Hair October Caddis, #14-18 Black Ant, #10-12 Foam Beetle, #8-12 Dave's Hopper.

Nymphs: #22-28 Midge Pupa, #22-28 Brassie, #22-28 Serendipity, #22-28 WD-40, #18 Black Stonefly Nymph, #16-18 Black Caddis Pupa, #12-22 Pheasant Tail Nymph, #16-18 Dun and Yellow Caddis Pupa, #14 Quill Gordon Nymph, #16 Blue Dun Nymph, #22-24 BWO Nymph, #14 March Brown Nymph, #14 Dark Hare's Ear Nymph, #14-16 Dark Hendrickson Nymph, #16 Dun and Green Caddis Pupa, #16 Olive Hare's Ear Nymph, #16-18 Sulphur Nymph, #16 Yellow Stonefly Nymph, #10 Green Drake Nymph, #14 Light Cahill Nymph, #14-18 Hare's Ear Nymph, #12 Yellow Drake Nymph, #12 Ginger Caddis Pupa, #14-16 Hardbody Ant, #8-12 Woolly Worm.

Streamers: #6-10 Krystal Bugger, #6-10 Woolly Bugger, #6-10 Muddler Minnow, #8 White Beadhead Flash Zonker, #8 Zonker, #6-10 Mickey Finn, #6-10 Black-nosed Dace.

When to Fish

The closer you get to McCaysville, the warmer the water gets. For the majority of the year, this isn't a concern. But during hot summers, the fishing can slow as a result of rising temperatures.

Seasons & Limits

The Toccoa tailwater is open to fishing all year and is under general regulations.

Nearby Fly Fishing

Jones Creek, Noontootla Creek, trophy-managed Noontootla Creek Farms, the upper Toccoa including the Toccoa delayed harvest, Blue Ridge Reservoir, and plenty of other small streams are all within a short drive of this section of the tailwater.

Accommodations & Services

Unicoi Outfitters in Blue Ridge runs plenty of float trips on the Toccoa tailwater, as does Reel Job Fishing Guide Service, Reel Angling Adventures, Southeastern Anglers, and Feather & Fly. The only fly shop in the area is Unicoi Outfitters in Blue Ridge.

Helpful Information

FeatherandFly.com
GoFishGeorgia.com
Kent-Klewein.com
ReelAnglingAdventures.com
SoutheasternAnglers.com
UnicoiOutfitters.com

TVA (Water Release Information): (800) 238-2264

Rating

This section of the Toccoa offers some very good fishing. I give it an 8 out of 10.

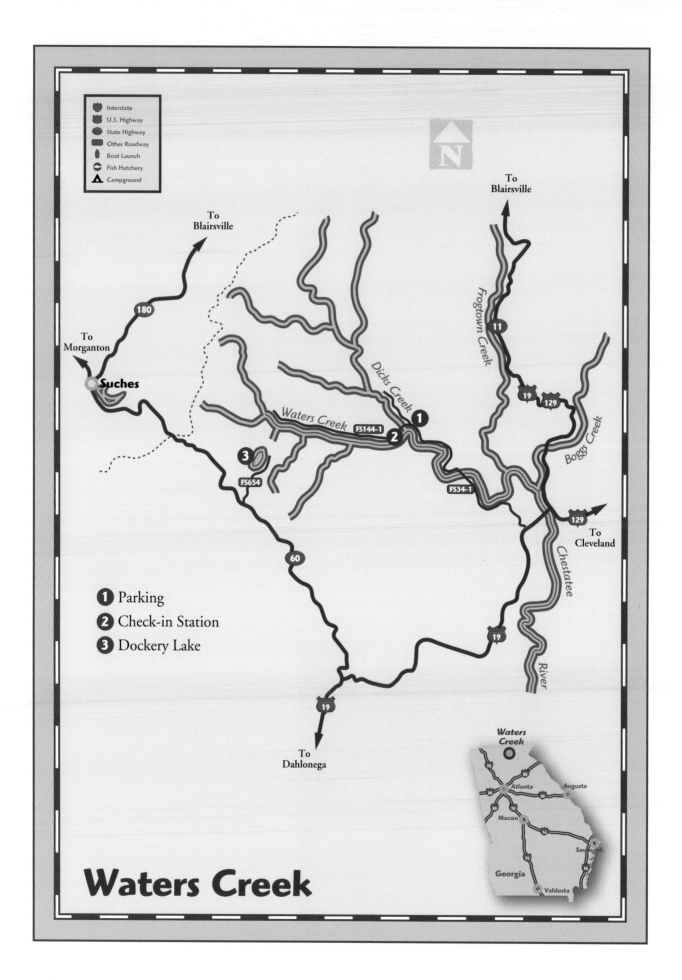

Legend:
- Interstate
- U.S. Highway
- State Highway
- Other Roadway
- Boat Launch
- Fish Hatchery
- Campground

To Blairsville

To Blairsville

Frogtown Creek

180

To Morganton

Suches

Waters Creek

Dicks Creek

FS144-1

1

2

11

19

129

Boggs Creek

FS654

3

FS34-1

129

To Cleveland

Chestatee River

60

1 Parking
2 Check-in Station
3 Dockery Lake

19

19

To Dahlonega

Waters Creek

Atlanta
Augusta
Macon
Savannah
Georgia
Valdosta

Waters Creek

Waters Creek

People say that Waters Creek is only a shadow of its former self. The glory days are long gone, they say. There aren't nearly as many trophy fish as there used to be, they say. You'd be better off going to Dukes Creek, they say.

And they're right. After a major poaching incident in the late '80s, a damaging tornado in the early '90s, the Blizzard of '93 and one heck of a flood in '94, Waters was left as a shell of its former self. But regardless, every time I've ever fished Waters Creek, the anticipation I feel during the drive there almost eats me alive.

Upon reaching Forest Service Road 34-1, it feels like you have arrived. However, once you're on that road, you still have to drive alongside Dicks Creek, stopping along the way to drool over the huge trout that reside in some of the privately owned stretches of the creek. By the way, you can't cast to those fish unless you have a fondness for the inside of a jail cell or a goal of making the "Hall of Shame" page in the next issue of *Georgia Outdoor News*. After gawking for a few minutes, you continue until the paved road turns to gravel, reach the parking area, pay the parking fee, check in at the Ranger station and hike up Forest Service Road 144-1.

The journey beginning with the turn onto Forest Service 34-1 and ending with a step into the cool flow of Waters Creek probably only takes about 15 minutes, but it definitely feels longer.

Types of Fish
Rainbow and brown trout.

Known Hatches
Small Dun Caddis, Blue-Winged Olive, Blue Quill Mayfly, Midges, Winter Black Stonefly, Quill Gordon Mayfly, Light Cahill Mayfly, Early Black Stonefly, Cream Caddis, Red Quill/Hendrickson, March Brown Mayfly, Yellow Stonefly, Golden Stonefly, Speckled Grey Caddis, Giant Black Stonefly, Sulphur Mayfly.

Equipment to Use
Rods: 3-5 weight, 7 to 8½ feet in length.

Reels: Standard disc drag.

Lines: Floating weight-forward or double-taper to match rod weight.

Leaders: Clear water—5X-6X leaders, 9 to 12 feet in length. Stained water—0X-3X leaders, 5 to 7 feet in length.

Wading: Hip- or waist-high waders work in low-water conditions. After a shower or during wetter years, chest waders should be worn. May through September means wet-wading here.

Flies to Use
Dry Flies: #16-20 Elk Hair Caddis, #16-18 BWO, #16-22 Adams, #16-22 Adams Parachute, #16-20 Adams Irresistible, #18-22 Griffith's Gnat, #16-18 Blue Quill, #16-22 Light Cahill Dun, #16-22 Light Cahill Parachute, #14-18 Yellow Stimulator, #16-20 Royal Wulff, #16-20 Royal Trude.

Continued

While Waters Creek is a trophy-managed stream, it is also home to an abundance of smaller wild fish.

Richie Santiago displays a 21-inch Waters Creek rainbow trout. Photo by David Cannon.

Pheasant Tail Nymph

I usually spend that time strategizing on how to sneak up on one of the bruisers in the glassy water just above the beaver dam where the road leaves the creek. My diabolical schemes never work, but I always convince myself that this will be the trip that it happens. And fortunately, two-and-a-half more miles of trophy-managed creek surround that 100-foot stretch of impossible water.

While Waters is not Dukes Creek, it does share aspects of Dukes that allow for some great experiences here. Since the poaching incidents and string of natural disasters, Waters has been in a sort of perpetual "rebuilding year," not unlike our Atlanta Hawks. But, an annual workday in September—The Waters Creek "Grunt and Groan"—led by angler Michael Pinion has added a lot of quality holding spots for the resident fish. There are decent numbers of 18- to 22-inch fish in some of the bigger pools and undercut banks at Waters, but nowhere near the amount Dukes boasts.

The key to having fun at Waters is managing your expectations. If a Noontootla Creek type of experience is one that you love, then think of Waters as a slightly-smaller version of Noontootla with a little bit of Dukes flavor mixed in. What I mean is, the majority of the fish you'll catch in Waters are small, wild rainbows—an absolute blast to go after with a slinky three-weight. But, there is always a chance that a drift through a deep hole or a swing-and-strip past an undercut bank could result in a hook-up with a fish that could turn a three-piece rod into a four-piece rod in a hurry.

Guide Julian Byrd battles a Waters Creek rainbow.

Flies to Use (continued)
Nymphs & Wet Flies: #14-16 Y2K Bug, #14-16 Glo Egg, #14-16 San Juan Worm, #12-20 Prince Nymph, #12-20 Hare's Ear Nymph, #12-16 Zug Bug, #8-20 Pheasant Tail, #16-18 Grey Caddis Pupa, #18-22 Midge Pupa, #16-20 Black Stonefly Nymph, #14-16 Yellow Stonefly Nymph, #4-8 Golden Stonefly Nymph, #4-8 Black Stonefly Nymph, #18-22 Disco Midge, #18-22 Zebra Midge, #16-22 Soft Hackle Wet, #16-22 Soft Hackle Pheasant Tail Nymph, #18-22 Lightning Bug, #18-20 Rainbow Warrior.

Streamers: #6-12 Krystal Bugger, #6-12 Woolly Bugger, #6-12 Muddler Minnow, #4-8 White Beadhead Flash Zonker, #4-8 Zonker, #4-10 Conehead Double Bunny, #6-8 Clouser Minnow, #6-10 Mickey Finn.

When to Fish
Like Dukes Creek, the big boys at Waters are much easier to entice when water visibility is low, therefore keeping the angler out of sight. So, watch for rain in the forecast and get to Waters when there is enough precipitation to create these conditions. Of course, spring and fall are great for fishing here, but this small creek also stays cool throughout the summer.

Seasons & Limits
Waters Creek is a seasonal stream that is open from 6:30 AM to 6:30 PM on Wednesdays, Saturdays and Sundays. Anglers must possess a fishing license, a trout stamp, and a WMA stamp in order to be legal here and only one artificial fly or lure with a single barbless hook not larger than a size six may be fished at a time (no droppers). Landing nets may not exceed two feet in length and anglers are allowed to keep one trout per day and no more than three trout per season; brook trout must have a minimum length of 18 inches and brown and rainbow trout must have a minimum length of 22 inches in order to be harvested. All other fish must be released immediately.

Nearby Fly Fishing
Waters Creek flows into Dicks Creek, a popular put-and-take fishery where large trout are harvested every season. Be sure not to trespass on the private waters of Dicks Creek. A trophy section on the Chestatee River, Frog Hollow, is nearby and Dukes Creek is only a 20-minute drive away.

Accommodations & Services
There are some nice campsites alongside Dicks Creek and hotels are available in the surrounding towns of Blairsville, Dahlonega, and Helen.

Helpful Web Site
NGTO.org

Rating
Waters offers anglers the chance to catch large quantities of small wild rainbows and a few trophy trout all on the same creek. This diversity makes it a 7 out of 10.

Carter Morris fishes just below the
Steele Bridge on Amicalola Creek

Delayed Harvest Trout Waters

The last Saturday of March in Georgia, or the opening day of trout season, used to be the most exciting day of the year for the masses with a trout stamp on their fishing licenses. That was then. This is now.

The first day of November marks the opening of Georgia's "second trout season," also known as delayed harvest, and anglers across north Georgia are bursting at the seams come mid-October in anticipation of the added opportunities.

Our Department of Natural Resources (DNR) defines this special season: "Delayed Harvest (DH) is a popular management strategy designed to provide a high quality catch and release trout fishery from fall through spring, after which the stream is opened for harvest under general regulations."

More specifically, from November 1 through May 14, stretches of water on two creeks and three rivers are managed as strictly catch and release, artificials-only fisheries. What's more is that they are absolutely loaded with fish! This makes for a perfect setting for those new to fly fishing and is also great fun for the experienced angler who simply wants to catch a lot of fish.

The delayed harvest program began in our state back in the 20th century—1996 to be exact—when the tiny tailrace of Smith Creek downstream of Unicoi Lake became the first stream here to have a portion of it designated as delayed harvest. After witnessing its popularity, a couple of years later the Georgia DNR decided that the stretch of Amicalola Creek from Steele Bridge Road, also marked as County Road 192, downstream to Georgia Highway 53, would be second in line for DH designation.

After that beginning, the Chattahoochee River through Atlanta received its own delayed harvest from the mouth of Sope Creek to U.S. Highway 41 some 3.7 miles downriver. The 2.3 miles of the upper Chattooga River from the mouth of Reed Creek down to the South Carolina Highway 28 bridge was the newest of Georgia's DH waters until 1.2 miles of the upper Toccoa River, south of Lake Blue Ridge, was opened for business in the fall of 2006. All of these streams are too warm for trout during the summer months, but, with the exception of Smith Creek, can be great for other species like shoal, redeye, or even smallmouth bass.

In addition to the large quantities of fish stocked at the beginning of DH season, the "fab five" of Georgia trout fishing usually receive monthly stockings to make up for fish lost to natural mortality or those who wander outside of DH boundaries and wind up on a plate next to some hush puppies.

Take a friend who has wanted to learn fly fishing to one of the following five locations. Each has its own unique qualities and challenges and each are great for introducing a newbie to this addiction.

Y2K Bug

The author's father, Jay Cannon, wades in the Toccoa River delayed harvest. Photo by David Cannon.

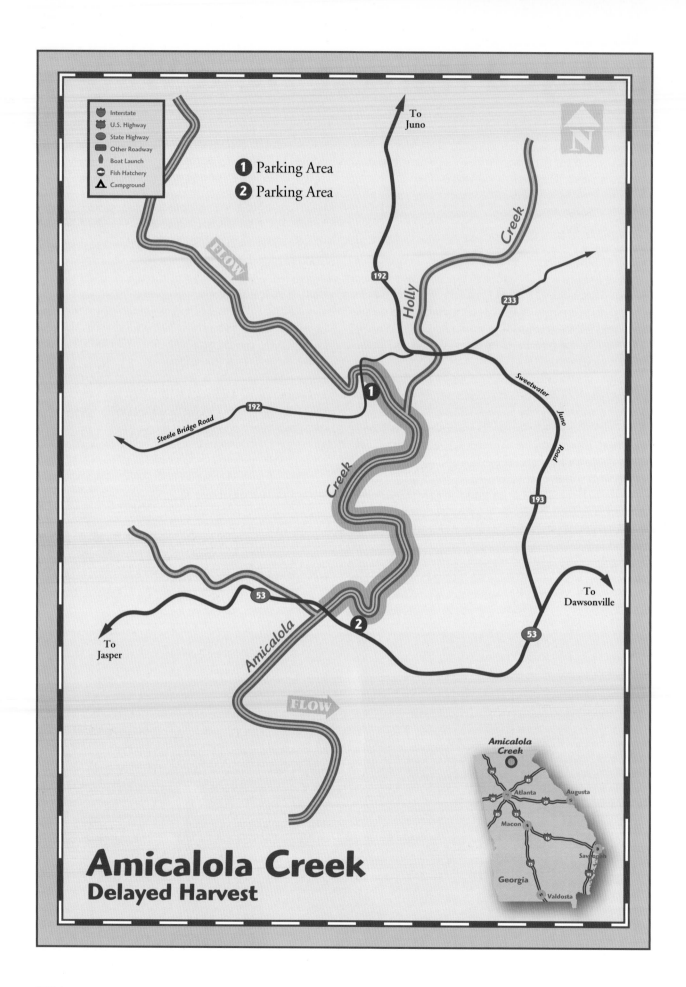

Legend
- Interstate
- U.S. Highway
- State Highway
- Other Roadway
- Boat Launch
- Fish Hatchery
- Campground

1 Parking Area
2 Parking Area

N

To Juno

Holly Creek

192

233

Sweetwater

FLOW

192

Steele Bridge Road

Creek

Juno Road

193

To Dawsonville

53

2

53

To Jasper

Amicalola

FLOW

Amicalola Creek
Delayed Harvest

Amicalola Creek

Georgia
75
85
Atlanta
Augusta
20
Macon
75
Savannah
75
Georgia
Valdosta

Amicalola Creek

Delayed Harvest

After the popularity of the Smith Creek Delayed Harvest became apparent, it was clear that there was a niche within the angling community for such regulated waters. So only a couple of years after Georgia's introduction to delayed harvest, more than three miles of Amicalola Creek, from Steele Bridge Road downstream to Georgia Highway 53, were designated as Georgia's second delayed harvest stream.

My favorite memory regarding the Amicalola DH is when my phone rang just after dark one spring evening and the caller ID displayed a good friend Andy Spencer's phone number. I knew I was about to hear a fishing story.

Any trout angler worth his or her salt knows to fish spring days until darkness has set as the half light usually provides a small window of opportunity—the "magic hour"—when a great hatch can occur or when the larger, more wary fish come out to feed. And on this night, Andy experienced this first hand.

Andy told me about how he had tangled with a monster rainbow trout just minutes before. His tale began with the strike indicator plunging below while fishing a very deep pool, then a drag-screaming run, and finally the heartbreak of a barbless hook flying back at him, prematurely ending the battle.

I received another phone call the very next night and thought for sure that Andy was pulling my leg when he said he had hooked this same fish again but was able to land it this time. The excitement in his voice seemed genuine as he talked of the amount of time the fish spent in the air during this fight. "It was like an obese man doing the high jump—exciting and scary all at the same time," Andy said. It wasn't until I saw the pictures that I knew for certain that he really did land this gigantic fish of 23 inches that weighed more than 8 pounds.

Types of Fish

Rainbow trout and, when the Federal hatchery makes too many, brook trout are stocked here for DH season. Brown trout are no longer stocked in this location because of their tendency to snack on a rare darter found in the creek. Redeye bass and redbreast sunfish make for fun action on the fly rod after the water gets too warm for trout.

Known Hatches

Small Dun Caddis, Blue-Winged Olive, Blue Quill Mayfly, Midges, Winter Black Stonefly, Quill Gordon Mayfly, Light Cahill Mayfly, Early Black Stonefly, Cream Caddis, Red Quill/Hendrickson, March Brown Mayfly, Yellow Stonefly, Golden Stonefly, Speckled Grey Caddis, Giant Black Stonefly, Sulphur Mayfly, Brown & Slate Drake Mayfly, Green Drake Mayfly, Coffin Fly (Green Drake Spinner).

Equipment to Use

Rods: 3-6 weight, 8-½ to 10 feet in length.
Reels: Standard disc drag.
Lines: Floating to match rod weight.
Leaders: 4X-6X leaders, 9 feet in length.
Wading: Chest waders should be used October through April. Spring and summer calls for wet-wading.

Flies to Use

Dry Flies: #12-18 Brown Elk Hair Caddis, #16-18 BWO, #8-22 Adams, #12-22 Adams Parachute, #12-18 Adams Irresistible, #18-22 Griffith's Gnat, #16-18 Blue Quill, #12-14 Quill Gordon, #16-20 Black Elk Hair Caddis, #14-16 Red Quill or Hendrickson, #12-14 Cream Elk Hair Caddis, #12-14 Light Cahill Dun, #12-14 Light Cahill Parachute, #14-16 Yellow Stimulator, #14-18 Sulphur Comparadun.

Nymphs: #14-16 Y2K Bug, #14-16 Glo Egg, #14 San Juan Worm, #12-18 Prince Nymph, #12-20 Hare's Ear, #12-16 Zug Bug, #8-20 Pheasant Tail, #16-18 Soft Hackle Pheasant Tail, #16-18 Grey Caddis Pupa, #18-22 Midge Pupa, #16-20 Black Stonefly Nymph, #4-8 Golden Stonefly Nymph, #8-14 March Brown Nymph, #4-8 Black Stonefly Nymph, #14-18 Sulphur Nymph or Emerger.

Streamers: #6-12 Woolly Bugger, #6-12 Muddler Minnow.

When to Fish

Any time you get a chance, but particularly during the week when the crowds are at work.

Seasons & Limits

From November 1 through May 14 of each year, this particular section falls under delayed harvest regulations—fishing with artificial lures and flies only, all catch and release, and only single hooks allowed. See the Georgia Sport Fishing Regulations booklet for more information.

Nearby Fly Fishing

Wildcat Creek is a great place to chase wild rainbows and Lake Sidney Lanier offers the chance at a striper or spotted bass on the fly.

Accommodations & Services

There isn't a convenient fly shop, so grab everything you need before heading in this direction.

Helpful Web Sites

FlyBoxOutfitters.com
GeorgiaFishingBooks.com
GoFishGeorgia.com
NGTO.org
TheFishHawk.com

Rating

Plenty of water that is rarely crowded combined with lots of fish throughout warrants a solid 8 out of 10.

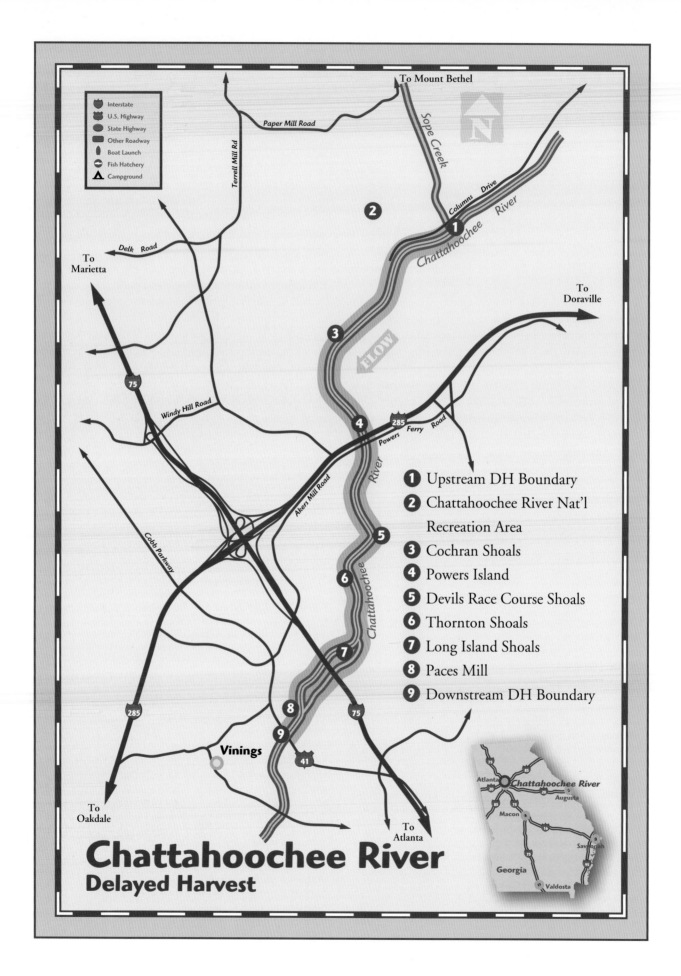

Legend:
- Interstate
- U.S. Highway
- State Highway
- Other Roadway
- Boat Launch
- Fish Hatchery
- Campground

To Mount Bethel

Paper Mill Road

Sope Creek

Terrell Mill Rd

Columns Drive

Chattahoochee River

N

Delk Road

To Marietta

To Doraville

FLOW

75

Windy Hill Road

285

Powers Ferry Road

River

Akers Mill Road

Cobb Parkway

Chattahoochee

1. Upstream DH Boundary
2. Chattahoochee River Nat'l Recreation Area
3. Cochran Shoals
4. Powers Island
5. Devils Race Course Shoals
6. Thornton Shoals
7. Long Island Shoals
8. Paces Mill
9. Downstream DH Boundary

285

75

8

9

41

Vinings

To Oakdale

To Atlanta

Chattahoochee River
Delayed Harvest

Georgia inset map: Atlanta, Chattahoochee River, Augusta, Macon, Savannah, Valdosta, Georgia

Chattahoochee River

Delayed Harvest

The third stream section to find itself in Georgia's delayed harvest program is also the largest. At 3.7 miles long and a few hundred feet wide, there's enough water here and enough trout stocked in this location to keep large numbers of Atlanta fly anglers happy.

The 'Hooch DH begins at the mouth of Sope Creek, which can be reached via Columns Drive. From there, the river flows over Cochran Shoals, an area of interest both for trout fishing and, when the weather is warmer, pursuing the voracious shoal bass. Continuing downstream, keep an eye out for stripers holding between Devils Race Course Shoals and Thornton Shoals. You might want to have something sturdier than the trusty five-weight in case you have such an encounter.

The area between I-285 and I-75 offers a lot of wadeable water and plenty of fish, but there are usually quite a few anglers crowding the area, as well. Passing under the I-75 bridge and continuing down to the Paces Mill area offers more waters densely populated with trout, many shoal areas where shoal bass can be targeted and, underneath the Highway 41 bridge, another chance at spotting a striper or two.

Perhaps the best way to explore the entire DH or certain stretches of it is to hop in a pontoon, canoe, kayak, or float tube (always with a personal floatation device) and anchor and fish all of the great water available. It takes about four and a half hours to float the entire DH, but floats can be made from one access point to the next in under an hour. Of course, this does not include fishing times.

Types of Fish

Rainbow and brown trout are the most abundant fish in the area. But, don't leave your bass outfit and flies at home. Shoal bass and stripers can be found here and will eat a fly.

Known Hatches

Midges, Black Stoneflies, Little Yellow Stoneflies, Black Caddis, Gray Caddis, Olive Caddis, Tan Caddis, October Caddis, Quill Gordon, Blue Dun, Blue-Winged Olive, March Brown, Hendrickson, Sulphurs, Green Drake, Light Cahill, Yellow Drake, Terrestrials.

Equipment to Use

Rods: 3-8 weight, 8½ to 10 feet in length (3-5 weight rods for trout, 5-6 weights for shoal bass and 7-8 weights for stripers).
Reels: A click-and-pawl reel is fine for most of the trout, but a reel with a disc drag is probably a smarter choice in case you run into a striper, shoal bass or larger trout.
Lines: Floating to match rod weight.
Leaders: 4X-6X leaders, 9 feet in length for trout; 1X-4X, 7½ feet long for shoal bass; 7½- to 9-foot leaders tapered to 16- or 20-pound test for stripers.
Wading: This is big water and is usually very cool. Stick to chest waders.

Flies to Use

Dry Flies: #22-28 Morgan's Para Midge, #18 Lowe's Little Dark Stonefly, #16-18 Black Elk Hair Caddis, #16-18 Gray Elk Hair Caddis, #14 Quill Gordon, #16 Blue Dun, #22-24 Parachute BWO, #14 Eastern March Brown, #14-16 Dark Hendrickson, #16 Olive Elk Hair Caddis, #16-18 Sulphur Comparadun, #16 North Carolina Yellow Sally, #10 Coffin Fly, #14 Parachute Light Cahill, #16-18 Tan Elk Hair Caddis, #12 Jim Charlie Classic, #14 Black Ant, #10 Foam Beetle, #10 Dave's Hopper, #12 Elk Hair Caddis, #12-22 Parachute Adams, #12-16 Stimulator.

Nymphs: #22-26 Midge pupa, #22-26 Brassie, #22-26 Serendipity, #22-26 WD-40, #18 Black Stonefly Nymph, #16-18 Black Caddis Pupa, #16-24 Pheasant Tail Nymph, #16-18 Soft Hackle Pheasant Tail, #16-18 Dun and Yellow Caddis Pupa, #14 Quill Gordon Nymph, #16 Blue Dun Nymph, #22-24 BWO Nymph, #14 March Brown Nymph, #14 Dark Hare's Ear Nymph, #14-16 Dark Hendrickson Nymph, #16 Dun and Green Caddis Pupa, #16 Olive Hare's Ear Nymph, #16-18 Sulphur Nymph, #16 Yellow Stonefly Nymph, #10 Green Drake Nymph, #14 Light Cahill Nymph, #16-18 Tan Caddis Pupa, #12 Yellow Drake Nymph, #14 Hardbody Ant, #10 Woolly Worm, #12 Ginger Caddis Pupa, #14-16 Y2K Bug, #14-16 Glo Egg, #14 San Juan Worm, #12-18 Prince Nymph, #12-20 Hare's Ear, #12-16 Zug Bug, #16-20 Rooks's Berry Nymph.

Streamers: #6-12 Woolly Bugger, #6-12 Muddler Minnow, #2-4 Clouser Minnow.

Poppers (for shoal bass): #2-4 DP Popper, #2-4 DP Slider, #4-6 Pencil Popper, #4-6 Kent's Stealth Bomber.

When to Fish

Fishing can be great anytime because of the sheer numbers of freshly-stocked fish present here.

Seasons & Limits

From November 1 through May 14 of each year, this particular section falls under delayed harvest regulations—fishing with artificial lures and flies only, all catch and release, and only single hooks allowed. See the Georgia Sport Fishing Regulations booklet for more information.

Nearby Fly Fishing

Rottenwood Creek, which runs along I-75, is known to hold rainbows looking to spawn in March and April. Besides that, you can chase carp in Bull Sluice Lake or trout, stripers, and shoal bass on other sections of the 'Hooch.

Accommodations & Services

You can hire a guide from River Through Atlanta Guide Service and get all of the gear you need to find success here from either Fly Box Outfitters in Kennesaw or The Fish Hawk in Atlanta.

Helpful Web Sites

FlyBoxOutfitters.com
GoFishGeorgia.com
NGTO.org
RiverThroughAtlanta.com
TheFishHawk.com

Rating

Wading the DH during rush hour makes this a 10 relative to what the rest of the Atlantans are doing at the time! The rest of the time, it's still an 8 out of 10 or better.

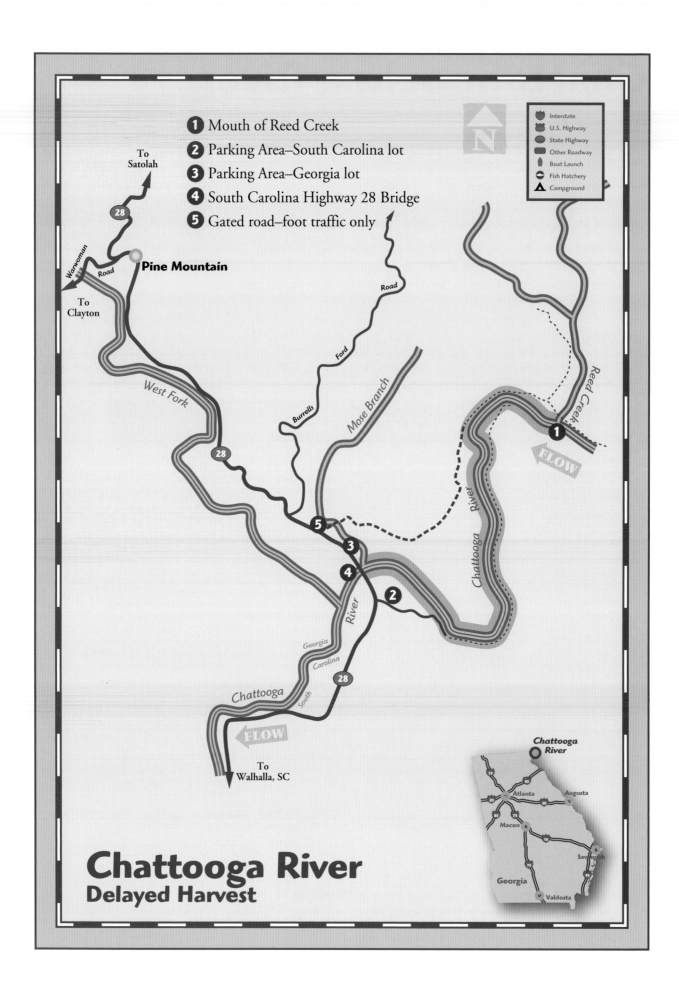

1 Mouth of Reed Creek
2 Parking Area–South Carolina lot
3 Parking Area–Georgia lot
4 South Carolina Highway 28 Bridge
5 Gated road–foot traffic only

Interstate
U.S. Highway
State Highway
Other Roadway
Boat Launch
Fish Hatchery
Campground

N

To Satolah

28

Warwoman Road

Pine Mountain

To Clayton

West Fork

28

Burrells

Mose Branch

Ford Road

Reed Creek

1

FLOW

Chattooga River

5

3

4

2

Georgia

Carolina

River

28

South

Chattooga

FLOW

To Walhalla, SC

Chattooga River
Delayed Harvest

Chattooga River

75
Atlanta
Augusta
85
75
Macon
16
Georgia
Savannah
95
Valdosta

Chattooga River

Delayed Harvest

Wildlife Resources Division Regional Fisheries supervisor and dedicated mentor of many anglers, Jeff Durniak, took me to this section for many of my early learning trips. It was here that I really began to love everything that fly fishing has to offer. I caught my first brown trout on a dry fly, my first brook trout, and, during a particularly good day, my first double here—two rainbows at the same time on two dry flies. Likewise, it is also the place I take friends on their first fly fishing expedition.

This delayed harvest water runs from the mouth of Reed Creek downstream 2.3 miles to the South Carolina Highway 28 Bridge, where parking is available on both sides of the river. Keep in mind that the 28 Bridge is also significant because it serves as the boating boundary—the river corridor above the bridge is zoned for foot travel only. Along this stretch are easy trails, great numbers of trout, and classic Chattooga scenery. Visit on a weekday and you're likely to experience some wonderful solitude as well.

Also, in the warmer months, don't be surprised if a beautiful redbreast attacks your dry fly or if an aggressive redeye bass strikes a Woolly Bugger stripped through shoals or deep holes. While some anglers would rather catch nothing but trout, a day of 20 to 30 trout with a few bonus redbreasts and redeye bass in this gorgeous setting sounds ideal to me.

Types of Fish
Rainbow, brown, and brook trout are abundant here from November 1 through May 14 every year. Like the Amicalola DH, redeye bass and redbreast sunfish also make for fun action on the fly rod.

Known Hatches
Small Dun Caddis, Blue-Winged Olive, Blue Quill Mayfly, Midges, Winter Black Stonefly, Quill Gordon Mayfly, Light Cahill Mayfly, Early Black Stonefly, Cream Caddis, Red Quill/Hendrickson, March Brown Mayfly, Yellow Stonefly, Golden Stonefly, Speckled Grey Caddis, Giant Black Stonefly, Sulphur Mayfly, Brown & Slate Drake Mayfly, Green Drake Mayfly, Coffin Fly (Green Drake Spinner).

Equipment to Use
Rods: 3-6 weight, 8½ to 10 feet in length.
Reels: A reel with a click-and-pawl or disc drag.
Lines: Floating to match rod weight.
Leaders: 4X-7X leaders, 9 to 12 feet in length.
Wading: Chest waders should be used October through April. May through September is prime time for wet-wading.

Flies to Use
Dry Flies: #12-18 Brown Elk Hair Caddis, #16-18 BWO, #8-22 Adams, #12-22 Adams Parachute, #12-18 Adams Irresistible, #18-22 Griffith's Gnat, #16-18 Blue Quill, #12-14 Quill Gordon, #16-20 Black Elk Hair Caddis, #14-16 Red Quill or Hendrickson, #12-14 Cream Elk Hair Caddis, #12-14 Light Cahill Dun, #12-14 Light Cahill Parachute, #14-16 Yellow Stimulator, #14-18 Sulphur Comparadun, #8-10 Green Drake, #8-10 Spent Wing or Parachute Coffin Fly.

Nymphs: #14-16 Y2K Bug, #14-16 Glo Egg, #14 San Juan Worm, #12-18 Prince Nymph, #12-20 Hare's Ear, #12-16 Zug Bug, #8-20 Pheasant Tail, #16-18 Soft Hackle Pheasant Tail, #16-18 Grey Caddis Pupa, #18-22 Midge Pupa, #16-20 Black Stonefly Nymph, #12-14 Quill Gordon Nymph, #12-14 Cream Caddis Pupa, #12-14 Light Cahill Nymph, #12-14 Dun & Yellow Caddis Pupa, #14-16 Yellow Stonefly Nymph, #4-8 Golden Stonefly Nymph, #8-14 March Brown Nymph, #4-8 Black Stonefly Nymph, #14-18 Sulphur Nymph or Emerger, #8-10 Green Drake Nymph.

Streamers: #6-12 Woolly Bugger, #6-12 Muddler Minnow.

When to Fish
Fishing for trout can be very good any time during the DH season. However, the month of November, and March through the close of DH (May 14), see the most consistent action. For redeye bass and sunfish, May through September in this section offers consistently good fishing.

Seasons & Limits
This section of the Chattooga, like the rest of it, can be fished year-round. However, from November 1 through May 14 of each year, this particular section falls under delayed harvest regulations. See the Georgia Sport Fishing Regulations booklet for more information.

Nearby Fly Fishing
Fishing the West Fork of the Chattooga and the tributaries of both forks is always fun. Also, the Tallulah River in Rabun County and its tributaries are definitely worth exploring.

Accommodations & Services
There are plenty of stores and several hotels in the nearby town of Clayton. You can also find a great selection of flies and fly fishing equipment at either location of Reeves Hardware—one in downtown Clayton and the other in Dillard.

Helpful Web Sites
GoFishGeorgia.com
NGTO.org
RabunTU.com
ReevesAceHardware.com
UnicoiOutfitters.com

Rating
Good numbers of willing fish, beautiful scenery and easy access with a backcountry feel make the Chattooga River DH a great place to fish. For me, it's an easy 9 out of 10.

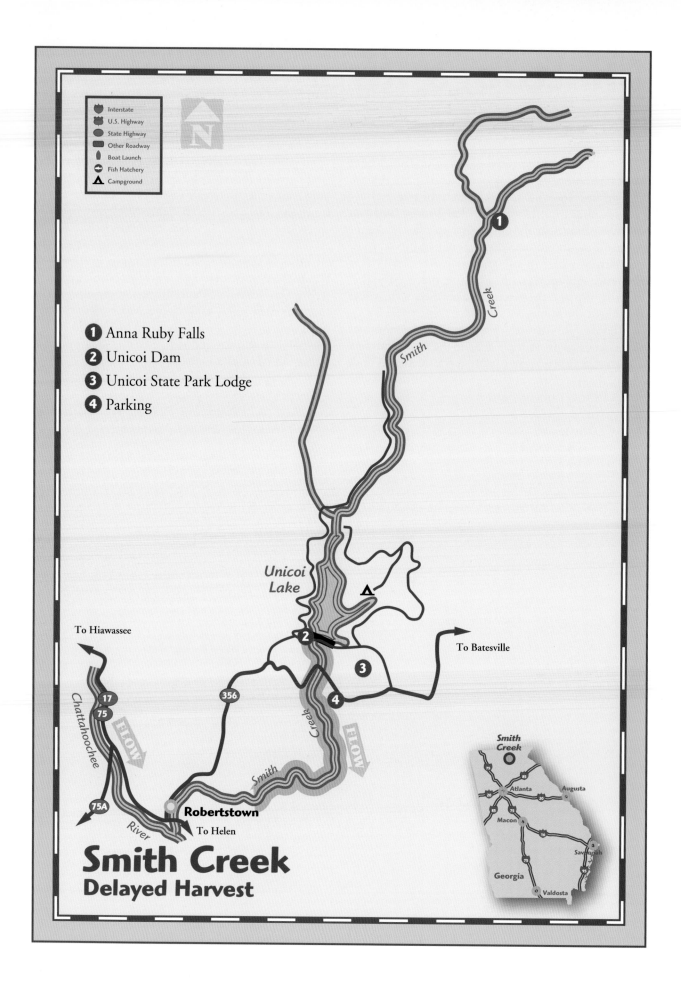

Legend:
- Interstate
- U.S. Highway
- State Highway
- Other Roadway
- Boat Launch
- Fish Hatchery
- Campground

N

1 Anna Ruby Falls
2 Unicoi Dam
3 Unicoi State Park Lodge
4 Parking

Smith Creek

Unicoi Lake

To Hiawassee

To Batesville

17
75

356

FLOW

FLOW

Chattahoochee

75A

River

Smith Creek

Robertstown

To Helen

Smith Creek
Delayed Harvest

Smith Creek

Atlanta
Augusta
Macon
Savannah
Georgia
Valdosta

Smith Creek

Delayed Harvest

The delayed harvest section of Smith Creek begins as the cold waters of Unicoi Lake pass through the dam and into a creek bed that averages only about ten feet in width. Combine its narrow width and its length of barely a mile, where it returns to the governance of general regulations at the Unicoi State Park property boundary, and this tiny tailwater makes up the smallest of Georgia's five DH trout waters.

Its diminutive size does not mean it should be overlooked. Smith is great training water for anglers of many different persuasions and, because of its relatively high fishing pressure, Smith can at times pose a challenge for even the most astute fly fisherman. It's a wonderful place to test small-stream tactics and techniques on less-educated stocker trout before visiting one of Georgia's many higher-elevation creeks teeming with fast and finicky wild fish. It also serves as a sort of gauge for anglers wishing to have success at nearby trophy stream, Dukes Creek. As a general rule of thumb, if you're not regularly catching at least a dozen fish on Smith, you probably have no business making reservations to fish Dukes. And consequently, if you happen to catch nothing but the proverbial skunk at Dukes, a quick trip across the valley to Smith afterwards will likely restore some level of confidence. Of course, I wouldn't know this from experience . . .

Because Smith is technically a tailwater, it generally runs clear even during or after a good rain. This characteristic calls for the use of light leaders (5X-7X). And, as most of this fishery is shallow, the majority of it can be effectively worked with a dry-dropper setup. Of course, don't hesitate to clip off the dry-dropper once you reach the culvert pool at the upper end. A few split-shot and a black leech dredged through its depths can produce some of the larger fish from this creek.

Types of Fish
Rainbows, browns, and brook trout are stocked here for DH season (brookies are stocked when the Federal hatchery has a surplus).

Known Hatches
It's rare to see enough mature insects hatching to cause the trout to look up. However, if you do see surface activity it's likely midges, light cahills or yellow sallies.

Equipment to Use
Rods: 3-5 weight, 7½ to 9 feet in length.
Reels: A click-and-pawl or disc drag reel.
Lines: Floating to match rod weight.
Leaders: 4X-6X leaders, 9 feet in length.
Wading: Because it's so small, waist-high waders suffice. Wet-wading is fine May through September.

Flies to Use
Dry Flies: #12-18 Brown Elk Hair Caddis, #16-18 BWO, #8-22 Adams, #12-22 Adams Parachute, #12-18 Adams Irresistible, #18-22 Griffith's Gnat, #16-18 Blue Quill, #12-14 Quill Gordon, #16-20 Black Elk Hair Caddis, #14-16 Red Quill or Hendrickson, #12-14 Cream Elk Hair Caddis, #12-14 Light Cahill Dun, #12-14 Light Cahill Parachute, #14-16 Yellow Stimulator, #14-18 Sulphur Comparadun.

Nymphs: #14-16 Y2K Bug, #14-16 Glo Egg, #14 San Juan Worm, #12-18 Prince Nymph, #12-20 Hare's Ear, #12-16 Zug Bug, #8-20 Pheasant Tail, #16-18 Soft Hackle Pheasant Tail, #16-18 Grey Caddis Pupa, #18-22 Midge Pupa, #16-20 Black Stonefly Nymph, #4-8 Golden Stonefly Nymph, #8-14 March Brown Nymph, #4-8 Black Stonefly Nymph, #14-18 Sulphur Nymph or Emerger.

Streamers: #6-12 Woolly Bugger, #6-12 Muddler Minnow.

When to Fish
After getting skunked at Dukes Creek, Smith is a great place to get your confidence back. Also keep in mind that because this is a tailwater creek, it runs relatively clear and calm during rainstorms when surrounding streams are blown out.

Seasons & Limits
From November 1 through May 14 of each year, this particular section falls under delayed harvest regulations—fishing with artificial lures and flies only, all catch and release, and only single hooks allowed. See the Georgia Sport Fishing Regulations booklet for more information.

Nearby Fly Fishing
The upper Chattahoochee River through and above Helen, Dukes Creek, and Nacoochee Bend are all within a five-minute drive.

Accommodations & Services
Rent a cabin, a room at the lodge, or camp out at Unicoi State Park and get all the gear you need from Unicoi Outfitters just south of Helen.

Helpful Websites
GoFishGeorgia.com
NGTO.org.
UnicoiOutfitters.com

Rating
Lots of stocked fish in a small-stream setting makes for a 7 out of 10.

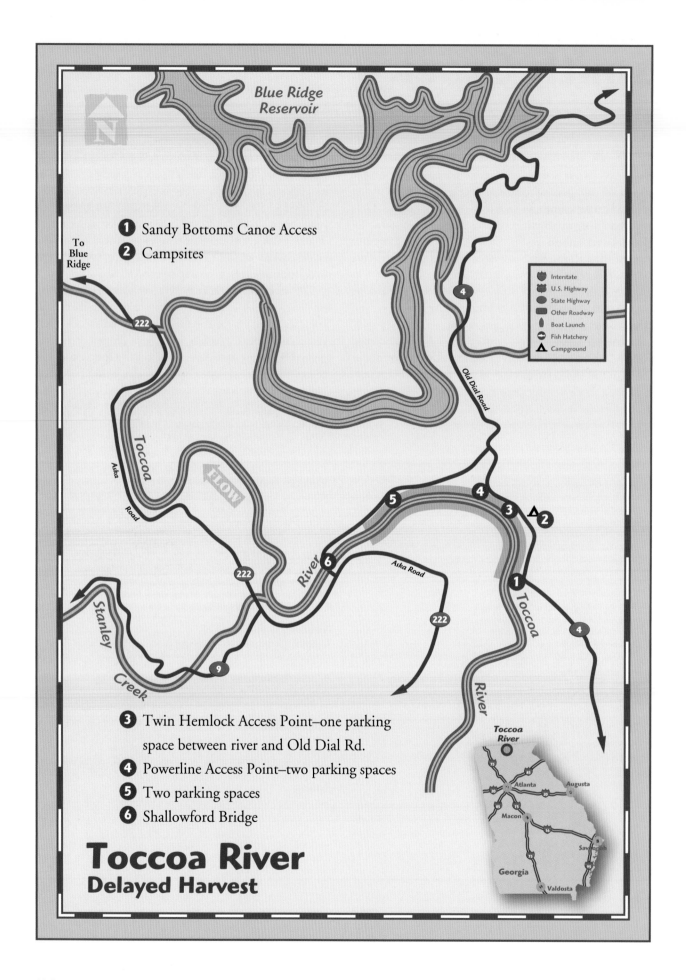

Blue Ridge Reservoir

① Sandy Bottoms Canoe Access

② Campsites

To Blue Ridge

Interstate
U.S. Highway
State Highway
Other Roadway
Boat Launch
Fish Hatchery
Campground

Toccoa
Aska Road
FLOW
River

Old Dial Road

③ Twin Hemlock Access Point–one parking space between river and Old Dial Rd.

④ Powerline Access Point–two parking spaces

⑤ Two parking spaces

⑥ Shallowford Bridge

Stanley Creek

Aska Road

Toccoa River

Toccoa River

Toccoa River
Delayed Harvest

Atlanta
Augusta
Macon
Savannah
Georgia
Valdosta

Toccoa River

Delayed Harvest

In 2006, the Georgia Wildlife Resources Division, the U.S. Forest Service, and the angling public agreed that a delayed harvest section on the upper Toccoa River would be a welcome addition to Georgia's already-diverse list of angling opportunities. The youngest of Georgia's five delayed harvest waters would reside on the upstream side of Blue Ridge Reservoir across a beautiful 1.2 mile length of freestone trout stream. Keep in mind, though, that upstream of the lake is also south as the river flows northward around Springer Mountain on its way into Tennessee.

This section is pretty tough wading, so the best way to experience the Toccoa DH is in the sitting position. Because of the relatively short float distance and the relatively high amount of fish-holding runs, eddies, and pools, a trip down this entire section in a pontoon or belly boat could take as little as two hours or as long as an entire day. It really just depends on how long each piece of water is fished.

This area is known for its healthy insect population and nice scenery. And, aside from the healthy DH trout to be found, there is also a chance at hooking into a smallmouth bass—an increasingly rare option in the Peach State. Smallies are native to the Toccoa River and, while their numbers are dwindling in much of their native ranges in Georgia because of competition from spotted bass, good numbers can still be found in Blue Ridge Reservoir and in the river itself.

Types of Fish
Brook, rainbow, and brown trout and the occasional smallmouth bass.

Equipment to Use
Rods: 3-6 weight rods, 8½ to 10 feet in length.
Reels: Standard disc drag.
Lines: Floating and intermediate lines to match rod weight.
Leaders: 3X-6X leaders, 9 feet in length for trout; 2X-4X leaders, 9 feet in length if targeting smallmouth.
Wading: As this is big water, chest waders should be worn for most of the DH season. The last few weeks of DH, however, might warrant wet-wading. Floating in a pontoon, canoe or belly boat down this stretch and anchoring to fish prime runs is the ticket for this water.

Flies to Use
Dry Flies: #12-18 Brown Elk Hair Caddis, #16-18 BWO, #8-22 Adams, #12-22 Adams Parachute, #12-18 Adams Irresistible, #18-22 Griffith's Gnat, #16-18 Blue Quill, #12-14 Quill Gordon, #16-20 Black Elk Hair Caddis, #14-16 Red Quill or Hendrickson, #12-14 Cream Elk Hair Caddis, #12-14 Light Cahill Dun, #12-14 Light Cahill Parachute, #14-16 Yellow Stimulator, #14-18 Sulphur Comparadun.

Nymphs: #14-16 Y2K Bug, #14-16 Glo Egg, #14 San Juan Worm, #12-18 Prince Nymph, #12-20 Hare's Ear, #12-16 Zug Bug, #8-20 Pheasant Tail, #16-18 Soft Hackle Pheasant Tail, #16-18 Grey Caddis Pupa, #18-22 Midge Pupa, #16-20 Black Stonefly Nymph, #4-8 Golden Stonefly Nymph, #8-14 March Brown Nymph, #4-8 Black Stonefly Nymph, #14-18 Sulphur Nymph or Emerger.

Streamers: #6-12 Woolly Bugger, #6-12 Muddler Minnow.

When to Fish
Like the other delayed harvest trout waters, the Toccoa section is great for trout throughout the entire DH season. During the warmer months, fewer trout will be around but smallmouth bass can be found and are great fun on fly tackle.

Seasons & Limits
From November 1 through May 14 of each year, this particular section falls under delayed harvest regulations—fishing with artificial lures and flies only, all catch and release, and only single hooks allowed. See the Georgia Sport Fishing Regulations booklet for more information.

Nearby Fly Fishing
The Toccoa River downstream of Blue Ridge Reservoir is one of the Southeast's best tailwater fisheries. Also nearby are Jones and Noontootla Creeks, which are two of the finest and most challenging of Georgia's wild trout waters. The private waters of Noontootla Creek Farms are also close and another option would be fishing Blue Ridge Reservoir for smallmouth bass.

Accommodations & Services
Unicoi Outfitters in Blue Ridge can set you up with a guide for this run and has all of the flies and tackle needed for the area. There are also plenty of cabins for rent in the Aska area.

Helpful Web Sites
BlueRidgeTu.com
GoFishGeorgia.com
NGTO.org.
UnicoiOutfitters.com

Rating
All of the delayed harvest streams should get at least a 7 out of 10 for their accessibility and catch rates. But, throw in the opportunity to catch a smallmouth for a few months of the year and this one gets a 9 out of 10.

Private Waters

Catch and Release Only

Fortunately for us all, the state of Georgia has public waters aplenty. However, some of the better-known trout streams and warmwater reservoirs can become a bit crowded, especially during the only times most of us can visit them—the weekends. But there is a way to beat the crowds and it's a pretty nice solution, too, if you have a little money in your pocket—paying a fee to gain access to some unbelievable waters that offer privacy and the possibility of a trophy catch.

Through careful management of all of these waters, the resident fish are often able to grow to enormous sizes. In some cases, fish weighing well into double-digit figures and measuring more than 30 inches have been caught.

I highly recommend all of the private waters that follow without any hesitation and hope you get a chance to experience all that they have to offer. Keep in mind that all of these locations have strict catch and release policies and, except Callaway Gardens, require fishing with barbless hooks.

Stephanie Cannon, Rex Gudgel, and Jimmy Harris display a fine rainbow caught at River North on the Soque River. Photo by David Cannon.

Barnsley Gardens

It's been said that there's no such thing as fun for the whole family. Barnsley Gardens proves that statement wrong. Since 2006, Barnsley Gardens has been an Orvis-Endorsed Lodge, offering a sporting clays course, bird hunts, a wing-shooting school, a fly fishing school, and some great access to fishing one of several lakes full of big bass and bream anxious to take a well-presented fly. Other options include golf, world-class dining, or a relaxing couple of hours at the spa. A fully-stocked fly shop on the grounds also has all of the gear and tackle one needs to have a successful trip here.

Contact:

597 Barnsley Gardens Rd.
Adairsville, GA 30103
(770) 773-7480
barnsleyresort.com

Guide Cody Jones scouts for one of the many large bass at Barnsley Gardens. Photo by David Cannon.

Brigadoon Lodge

Perhaps no private fishing operation in Georgia has received as much press and attention as Brigadoon Lodge, and with good reason. Brigadoon is situated on the picturesque Soque River and is saturated with gigantic fish. The lodge, which consists of three lodge houses, has 14 private bedrooms and plays host to the wonderful meals served at Brigadoon. Catering to individuals looking to get away, couples hoping for a romantic weekend, or full-scale corporate retreats are all well within their field of expertise. Fishing with a guide is required here unless you are a usual customer.

Contact: Rebekah Stewart
P.O. Box 2407
Clarkesville, GA 30523
(706) 754-1558
brigadoonlodge.com

Brigadoon is home to many very large trout.

The 39th President of the United States, Jimmy Carter, casting on the Soque River.

Callaway Gardens

If you like catching fish—namely big bass, huge bream, and even trout in the winter months—in the setting of an immaculately-manicured garden, then Callaway Gardens is the place for you.

Established in 1952 as the Ida Cason Gardens, Callaway can now boast of being one of the finest gardens in the Southeast. Its numerous lakes and ponds are all great for casting poppers, Kent Edmonds's Stealth Bombers, Clouser's Minnows, and Carter's Rubber-legged Dragons (RLDs).

Kingfisher Outfitters on the premises can set you up with a guide, flies, tackle, or even a boat. Lodging options include villas, cottages, an inn, and the main lodge, which also has a full-service spa. Eleven restaurants on location serve everything from southern classics to hand-spun malts. You can even play golf on one of their two courses, but who has time for that when there are two-pound bream nearby?

Contact: Kingfisher Outfitters
(706) 663-5142
callawaygardens.com

Left: Guide Kent Edmonds rows Stephanie Cannon around one of the many productive lakes at Callaway Gardens. Below: Kent Edmonds and Stephanie Cannon display one of the many rainbow trout that are stocked at Callaway each winter. Photos by David Cannon.

Frog Hollow

Barely more than an hour's drive from north Atlanta near the town of Dahlonega runs the picturesque Chestatee River. And in the valley called Frog Hollow runs a stretch of the river containing some of the biggest rainbows in all of north Georgia. Through this length there are a few shoals and rocky runs, but the majority of Frog Hollow is slick but steady water which is conducive to either a dry fly or a dry-dropper setup. Tempting a humongous trout to rise can be an option here almost any time of year. Spending time with a guide working this water is a lot of fun, but the icing on the cake at this location is the pool below the beautiful waterfall near the upper end of the property. This is the place to tie on a big nymph rigged to go deep, so set your drag and hang on!

Contact: Unicoi Outfitters—
Blue Ridge or Helen, GA
(706) 632-1880 or (706) 878-3083
unicoioutfitters.com

Guide and FFF Certified Master Casting Instructor Rex Gudgel prepares to make a long cast on the Chestatee River.

Nacoochee Bend

Just south of the town of Helen, Unicoi Outfitters manages one and a half miles of the upper Chattahoochee River as trophy water. "The Bend" is an awesome place to spend a morning, an afternoon or a full day chasing some truly large rainbows and browns. Fishing below the spillway right behind the historic Nora Grist Mill is a favorite spot for many who frequent the bend, but spending too much time there and not covering the rest of this great water would be a blunder. Several deep runs and bends are always completely full of fly-eating beasts, as are the rest of the waters here.

Trips to the bend can be taken with a guide or can be self-guided if the angler has fished this spot previously. Unicoi Outfitters also has a special deal that involves a free half-day of fishing the bend with the purchase of any premium fly rod—talk about a good excuse to buy a new rod!

Contact: Unicoi Outfitters
P.O. Box 419
7280 S. Main St.
Helen, GA 30545
(706) 878-3083
unicoioutfitters.com

Rodger Naugle with a very large Nacoochee Bend rainbow trout. Photo by David Cannon.

Noontootla Creek Farms

This trophy stream has the distinction of playing host to the Fly Fishing Masters Finals in 2006. Noontootla Creek Farms lies just south of Blue Ridge and downstream of the public section of heralded Noontootla Creek. Here the Owenby family has around 1,500 of the most beautiful acres of paradise you can imagine with more than two miles of the creek tumbling through it. The resident trophy and stream-born browns and rainbows, many of which surpass the 20-inch mark, present a nice challenge for even experienced anglers, all in a small-stream setting.

NCF also offers a top-notch sporting clays course and some great quail hunting. The "Cast and Blast," a half-day of fly fishing and a half-day of quail hunting, is a popular option here.

Contact:

Unicoi Outfitters
Blue Ridge, GA
490 East Main St.
Blue Ridge, GA 30513
(706) 632-1880
unicoioutfitters.com and ncfga.net

Reel Angling Adventures
(866) 899-5259
ReelAnglingAdventures.com

Reel Job Fishing
(770) 330-7583
Kent-Klewein.com

Standing at 6 feet 7 inches tall, Julian Byrd makes this stream bred brown trout appear smaller than it actually is. This magnificent fish was well over 20 inches long.

River North

Another private operation on the Soque River, River North, boasts of about a mile and a half of great water full of huge rainbows and browns. This portion of the Soque consists of river bend after river bend, meaning there is no shortage of holding water for the trophies that reside here. One particular point of interest is "the peninsula," which is a small finger of land surrounded by the Soque. One could spend an entire day working the water on this short stretch, but then would miss the rest of this great property. Trips to River North can be booked through Unicoi Outfitters or directly through River North.

Contact:

Unicoi Outfitters
P.O. Box 419
7280 S. Main St.
Helen, GA 30545
(706) 878-3083
unicoioutfitters.com

Eddie Michael
River North Fly Fishing
P.O. Box 2468
Clarkesville, GA 30523
(404) 403-2808
rivernorthflyfishing.com

Stephanie Cannon fights a large Soque River rainbow with the coaching of guide Rex Gudgel. Photo by David Cannon.

A great moment on a great stream in north Georgia, Dukes Creek. Photo by David Cannon.

Resources

Stores

This listing of resources is provided as a courtesy to help you enjoy your travels and fishing experience and is not intended to imply an endorsement of services either by the publisher or author. These listings are as accurate as possible as of the time of publication and are subject to change.

Alpharetta Outfitters
488 N. Main St.
Suite 109
Alpharetta, GA 30009
(678) 762-0057
alpharettaoutfitters.com

Bass Pro Shops
5900 Sugarloaf Pkwy
Lawrenceville, GA 30043
(678) 847-5500
basspro.com

Bass Pro Shops
5000 Bass Pro Blvd.
Macon, GA 31210
(478) 757-7600
basspro.com

Bass Pro Shops
14045 Abercorn St.
Savannah, GA 31419
(912) 961-4200
basspro.com

Bass Pro Shops
Augusta, GA
Store Opening Fall 2009
basspro.com

Broadway Tackle
1730 Broad St.
Augusta, GA 30904
(706) 738-8848
broadwaytackle.com

The Fish Hawk
3095 Peachtree Rd.
Atlanta, GA 30305
(800) 331-8919 or
(404) 237-3473
thefishhawk.com

Fly Box Outfitters
840 Ernest W Barrett Pkwy NW,
Suite 568
Kennesaw, GA 30144
(678) 594-7330
(866) 460-2507
flyboxoutfitters.com

Hammond's Fishing Center
4255 Browns Bridge Rd.
Cumming, GA 30041
(770) 888-6898
hammondsfishing.net

Highland Outfitters, LLC
175 Pine Grove Rd., Suite 215
Cartersville, GA 30120
(770) 387-9881
highlandoutfittersLLC.com

Kevin's of Thomasville
111 S. Broad St.
Thomasville, GA 31792
(229) 226-7766
kevinscatalog.com

Kingfisher Outfitters
17800 U.S. Highway 27
Pine Mountain, GA 31822
(706) 663-2281
callawaygardens.com

Lake Oconee Outfitters, Inc.
1093 Greensboro Rd.
Eatonton, GA 31024
(706) 923-0999
lakeoconeeoutfitters.com

Nature's Tackle Box
4215 Jimmy Lee Smith Pkwy,
Unit 12B
Hiram, GA 30141
(678) 567-1211

Orvis Buckhead
3275 Peachtree Rd. NE,
Suite 210
Buckhead Square
Atlanta, GA 30305
(404) 841-0093
orvis.com

Orvis The Forum
5161 Peachtree Pkwy NW,
Suite 630
Norcross, GA 30092
(770) 798-9983
orvis.com

Orvis Barnsley Gardens
597 Barnsley Gardens Rd.
Adairsville, GA 30103
(770) 773-9230
orvis.com
barnsleyresort.com

Reeves Ace Hardware
46 S. Main St.
Clayton, GA 30525
(706) 782-4253

Reeves Ace Hardware
7314 Highway 441 N
Dillard, GA 30537
(706) 746-7414

Rivers & Glen Trading Company
387 Highland Ave.
Augusta, GA 30909
(706) 738-4536
riversandglen.com

River Supply Inc.
2827 River Dr.
Savannah, GA 31404
(912) 354-7777

St. Simons Outfitters
3405 Frederica Rd.
St. Simons Island, GA 31522
(912) 638-5454
stsimonsoutfitters.com

Unicoi Outfitters
P.O Box 419
7280 S. Main St.
Helen, GA 30545
(706) 878-3083
unicoioutfitters.com

Unicoi Outfitters
490 E. Main St.
Blue Ridge, GA 30513
(706) 632-1880
unicoioutfitters.com

Guides

Legend:

FFF = Federation of Fly Fishers Certified Casting Instructor
FFFM = Federation of Fly Fishers Certified Master Casting Instructor
HYB = Hybrid Bass
LMB = Largemouth Bass
SH = Shoal Bass
SLT = Saltwater Species
SMB = Smallmouth Bass
SP = Spotted Bass
ST = Striped Bass
T = Trout

Guide Julian Byrd talks strategy with an angler before hitting the stream.

Action Flies (SP, ST)
Kevin Arculeo
Alpharetta, GA
(404) 386-4598
Kevin@actionflies.com
actionflies.com

Captain Guide Service (T)
Carter Morris
(706) 833-1303
cmorrisprivate@gmail.com

Captain Scott Owens (SLT)
St. Simons Island, GA
(877) 605-3474
scott@flyfishgeorgia.com
flyfishgeorgia.com

Chattahoochee River Outfitters (T)
(770) 402-7883
fourdawg@comcast.net
chatriveroutfitters.com

Henry Cowen Guide Service (SP, ST, FFF)
Cumming, GA
(678) 513-1934
henryc@pastourelledesign.com
henrycowenflyfishing.com

Fly Fishing West Georgia & Beyond (SH, ST, FFF)
Kent Edmonds
(706) 883-7700
kje@mindspring.com
flyfishga.com

Get Looped Fly Fishing (T, FFFM)
Rex Gudgel
(706) 254-3504
phishmoore@aol.com

Hildreth Charters (SLT)
Captain Greg Hildreth
Brunswick, GA
(912) 261-1763
goldenislesflyfishing.com

Nathan Lewis Guide Service (LMB, SMB, SP)
Lake Blue Ridge
(706) 633-0461

Reel Angling Adventures (T, SMB, SP, ST)
Suches, GA
(866) 899-5259
reelanglingadventures.com

Reel Job Fishing (T, SMB, SP, LMB)
Kent Klewein
Blue Ridge, GA
(770) 330-7583
Kent-Klewein.com

Reel Sports Guide Service (LMB, HYB, ST)
Captain Mike Sloan
Lake Seminole
(229) 246-0658
wingateslodge@bellsouth.net
sloanreelsports.com

River Through Atlanta Chattahoochee River Guide Service (T)
Chris Scalley
Roswell, GA
(770) 650-8630
riverthroughatlanta.com

St. Simons Outfitters (SLT)
St. Simons Island, GA
(912) 638-5454
stsimonsoutfitters.com

Savannah Fly Fishing Charters (SLT)
Captain Scott Wagner
Savannah, GA
(912) 308-3700
scott@savannahfly.com
savannahfly.com

Sweetwater Anglers (T)
Charles Henderson
Oakwood, GA
(770) 530-2228
sweetwateranglers.com

Unicoi Outfitters (T, SMB, SP, FFF, FFFM)
Blue Ridge, GA
(706) 632-1880
unicoioutfitters.com

Unicoi Outfitters (T, FFF, FFFM)
Helen, GA
(706) 878-3083
unicoioutfitters.com

Henry Williamson (T)
(706) 746-5631

This river house on the Toccoa is the home and shop of famed bamboo fly rod builder Bill Oyster and his family. Photo by Stephanie Cannon.

Fly Fishing Classes

Atlanta Fly Fishing School
Fly Fishing & Casting Classes
Atlanta, GA
(404) 550-6890
atlantaflyfishingschool.com

Callaway Gardens
Fly Fishing Classes
Pine Mountain, GA
(706) 663-5142
callawaygardens.com

The Fish Hawk/Sage Fly Fishing School
Fly Fishing & Tying Classes
Sky Valley, GA
(404) 237-3473
thefishhawk.com

Fly Box Outfitters
Fly Fishing & Tying Classes
Kennesaw, GA
(678) 594-7330
flyboxoutfitters.com

Orvis Fly Fishing School
Barnsley Gardens
Fly Fishing Classes
Adairsville, GA
(877) 773-2447
barnsleyresort.com

Unicoi Outfitters
Fly Fishing Classes, Fly Tying Classes
and the "Gilligan Special"
Blue Ridge and Helen, GA locations
(706) 632-1880
unicoioutfitters.com

Georgia Fly Fishing Art

Bucky Bowles
Fortson, GA
(706) 323-9781
buckybowles.com

Catch and Release Paintings by Paul Puckett
Atlanta, GA
(770) 378-7300
catchandreleasepaintings.com

Patsy Lewis-Gentry
Sautee, GA
(706) 878-4693
patsygentry@windstream.net

The Watercolor of Tom Landreth
(706) 746-2295
tomlandreth.com

Custom Rod Building

North Georgia Custom Rods
Mack Martin
Cumming, GA
(770) 889-5638
mackmartin.com

Oyster Fine Bamboo Fly Rods
Mineral Bluff, GA
(706) 374-4239
oystersb@mindspring.com
oysterbamboo.com

Conservation Groups & Fly Fishing Clubs

Atlanta Fly Fishing Club
Federation of Fly Fishers
Atlanta, GA
atlantaflyfishingclub.org

Chattahoochee Coldwater Fishery Foundation
chattahoocheefoodwebs.org

Coastal Conservation Association Georgia
42 W. Montgomery Crossroads,
Suite K
Savannah, GA 31406
(912) 927-0280
ccaga.org

Fall Line Fly Anglers
Macon, GA
falllineflyanglers.com

Georgia Trout Unlimited Back-the-Brookie
btb@georgiatu.org
georgiatu.org/html/back_the_brookie.html

Georgia Trout Unlimited Trout Camp
Boys and girls, 12-15 years old
georgiatu.org/html/trout_camp.html

Georgia Women Fly Fishers
Marietta, GA
georgiaflyfishing.com

North Georgia Trout Online (NGTO)
ngto.org

Trout Unlimited Chapters in Georgia

Blue Ridge Mountain Chapter
Blue Ridge, GA
blueridgetu.com

Chattahoochee/Nantahala Chapter
Blairsville, GA
ngatu692.com

Cohutta Chapter
Marietta, GA
tucohutta.org

Coosa Valley Chapter
Rome, GA
coosavalleytu.org

Flint River Chapter
Peachtree City, GA
flinttu.org

Georgia Foothills Chapter
Cornelia, GA
georgiafoothills.org

Gold Rush Chapter
Dahlonega, GA
goldrushtu.org

Kanooka Chapter
Snellville, GA
kanookatuga.org

Oconee River Chapter
Athens, GA
orctu.org

Rabun Chapter
Clayton, GA
rabuntu.com

Tailwater Chapter
Cumming, GA
tailwatertu.com

Upper Chattahoochee Chapter
Roswell, GA
ucctu.org

Other Useful Phone Numbers and Web sites

Army Corps of Engineers
Army Corps of Engineers reservoir maps
usace.army.mil

Buford Dam
Water release schedule
(770) 945-1466
water.sam.usace.army.mil

Georgia Power Company
Georgia Power reservoir maps
gapower.com

Georgia Wildlife Resources Division
Trout stream maps, fishing licenses, fishing predictions, etc.
gofishgeorgia.com

Morgan Falls Dam
(404) 329-1455

National Parks Service
Park maps
nps.gov

Tennessee Valley Authority
Blue Ridge Dam (Toccoa River Tailwater)
(800) 238-2264
Dial 4 then 23 for the Blue Ridge Dam release schedule
tva.gov/sites/blueridge.htm

United States Forest Service
Forest maps, recreational areas, etc.
fs.fed.us

United States Geological Survey
Water data (stream flows)
ga.water.usgs.gov

Supporting Trout Unlimited by joining a local chapter and getting involved is a wonderful idea.

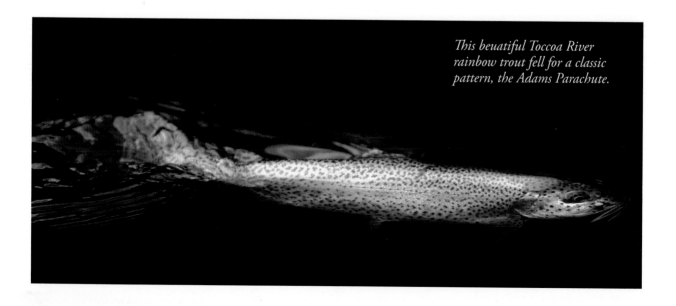

This beuatiful Toccoa River rainbow trout fell for a classic pattern, the Adams Parachute.

The thick vegetation and lily pads on the surface of Lake Seminole provide cover for big Georgia largemouths.

Guide Rex Gudgel poles his flats skiff in search of the wary carp. Photo by David Cannon.

Conservation

No Nonsense Fly Fishing Guidebooks believes that, in addition to local information and gear, fly fishers need clean water and healthy fish. We encourage preservation, improvement, conservation, enjoyment, and understanding of our waters and their inhabitants. While fly fishing, take care of the place, practice catch and release, and try to avoid spawning fish.

When you aren't fly fishing, a good way to help all things wild and aquatic is to support organizations dedicated to these ideas. We encourage you to get involved, learn more, and to join such organizations.

American Rivers ....(202) 347-7550
Blackfoot Challenge ....(406) 793-9300
California Trout ....(415) 392-8887
Camo Coalition ....(770) 787-7887
Chattahoochee Coldwater Fishery Foundation ....(770) 650-8630
Coastal Conservation Association Georgia ....(912) 927-0280
Deschutes Basin Land Trust ....(541) 330-0017
Federation of Fly Fishers ....(406) 585-7592
Georgia Department of Natural Resources (Fisheries) ....(770) 918-6406
Georgia Outdoor Network ....(800) 866-5516
International Game Fish Association ....(954) 927-2628
International Women Fly Fishers ....(925) 934-2461
New Mexico Trout ....(505) 884-5262
Oregon Trout ....(503) 222-9091
Outdoor Writers Association of America ....(406) 728-7434
Recreational Fishing Alliance ....(888) JOIN-RFA
Rails-to-Trails Conservancy ....(202) 331-9696
Theodore Roosevelt Conservation Partnership ....(877) 770-8722
Trout Unlimited ....(800) 834-2419

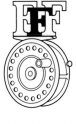

Find Your Way with These No Nonsense Guides

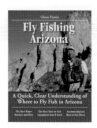 ### Fly Fishing Arizona
Glenn Tinnin
Desert, forest, lava fields, red rocks and canyons. Here is where to go and how to fish 32 cold and warm water streams, lakes, and reservoirs in Arizona. Newly revised.
ISBN 978-1-892469-02-1 .... $18.95

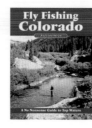 ### Fly Fishing Colorado
Jackson Streit
Your experienced guide gives you a quick, clear understanding of the information you'll need to fly fish Colorado's most outstanding waters. Use this book to plan your Colorado fly fishing trip, and take it along for ready reference. Full color.
ISBN 978-1-892469-13-7 .... $19.95

 ### Fly Fishing Southern Baja
Gary Graham
With this book you can fly to Baja, rent a car and go out on your own to find exciting saltwater fly fishing! Mexico's Baja Peninsula is now one of the premier destinations for saltwater fly anglers. Newly revised.
ISBN 978-1-892469-00-7 .... $18.95

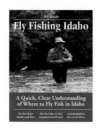 ### Fly Fishing Idaho
Bill Mason
The Henry's Fork, Salmon, Snake, and Silver Creek plus 24 other waters. Bill Mason shares his 30 plus years of Idaho fly fishing. Newly revised.
ISBN 978-1-892469-17-5 .... $18.95

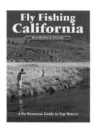 ### Fly Fishing California
Ken Hanley
Ken Hanley's vast experience gives you a clear understanding of the best places to fish across California—from the Baja coast to the northern wilderness. The redesigned and expanded version of Hanley's popular *Guide to Fly Fishing in Northern California*.
ISBN 978-1-892469-10-6 .... $28.95

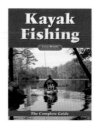 ### Kayak Fishing
Cory Routh
Routh covers everything you need for safe, fun, and successful kayak fishing. This guide gives you a quick, clear understanding of the essential information you will need to get started in this growing sport.
ISBN 978-1-892469-19-9 .... $24.95

 ### Fly Fishing the California Delta
Captain Mike Costello
The first major book describing the techniques for landing trophy striped bass and other species in the California Delta. Covers more than 2,000 levees and 1,200 miles of rivers. Full color. Hardcover.
ISBN 978-1-892469-23-6 .... $49.95

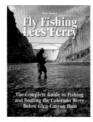 ### Fly Fishing Lees Ferry
Dave Foster
This guide provides a clear understanding of the complex and fascinating river that can provide fly anglers 40-fish days. Detailed maps show fly and spin fishing access. Learn about history, boating, and geology. Indispensable for the angler and intrepid visitor to the Marble Canyon.
ISBN 978-1-892469-15-1 .... $18.95

 ### Fishing Central California
Brian Milne
This comprehensive and entertaining guide will improve your chances when you cast a line in Central California and beyond. You'll learn where the best spots are on the streams, rivers, lakes, and ocean fisheries, how to change tactics, and select the right baits, lures, and equipment. Full color.
ISBN 978-1-892469-18-2 .... $24.95

 ### Fly Fishing Magdalena Bay
Gary Graham
Guide and excursion leader Gary Graham (*Baja On The Fly*) lays out the truth about fly fishing for snook in mangroves, and off-shore marlin. Photos, illustrations, maps, and travel information, this is "the Bible" for this unique region.
ISBN 978-1-892469-08-3 .... $24.95

Seasons of the Metolius
John Judy

This book describes how a beautiful riparian environment both changes and stays the same over the years. Mr. Judy makes his living in nature and chronicles his 30 years of study, writing, and fly fishing his beloved home water—the crystal clear Metolius River in central Oregon.
ISBN 978-1-892469-11-3 .... $20.95

Fly Fishing Pyramid Lake
Terry Barron

The Gem of the Desert is full of huge Lahontan Cutthroat trout. Terry has recorded everything you need to fly fish the most outstanding trophy cutthroat fishery in the U.S. Where else can you get tired of catching 18–25" trout?
ISBN 978-0-9637256-3-9 .... $15.95

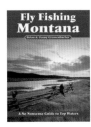

Fly Fishing Montana
Brian & Jenny Grossenbacher

Explore Montana—a fly angler's mecca—as Brian and Jenny Grossenbacher guide you through their beautiful home state. You'll get the information you need to fly fish Montana's outstanding waters.
ISBN 978-1-892469-14-4 .... $28.95

Fly Fishing Utah
Steve Schmidt

Utah yields extraordinary, uncrowded and little known fishing. Steve Schmidt, outfitter and owner of Western Rivers Fly Shop in Salt Lake City has explored these waters for over 28 years. Covers mountain streams and lakes, tailwaters, and reservoirs. Newly revised.
ISBN 978-0-9637256-8-4 .... $19.95

Fly Fishing Nevada
Dave Stanley

The Truckee, Walker, Carson, Eagle, Davis, Ruby, mountain lakes, and more. Mr. Stanley is recognized nationwide as the most knowledgeable fly fisher and outdoorsman in the state of Nevada. He owns and operates the Reno Fly Shop and Truckee River Outfitters in Truckee, California. Newly revised.
ISBN 978-0-9637256-2-2 .... $18.95

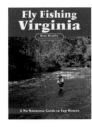

Fly Fishing Virginia
Beau Beasley

From urban streams to the Shenandoah National Park, Beau Beasley shows you where to fly fish in Virginia. Detailed maps, photographs, and Beasley's wisdom guide you through the many waters in the Old Dominion. Full color.
ISBN 978-1-892469-16-8 .... $28.95

Fly Fishing New Mexico
Taylor Streit

Since 1970, Mr. Streit has been New Mexico's foremost fly fishing authority and professional guide. He owned the Taos Fly Shop for ten years and managed a bone fishing lodge in the Bahamas. Taylor makes winter fly fishing pilgrimages to Argentina where he escorts fly fishers and explorers. Newly revised.
ISBN 978-1-892469-04-5 .... $18.95

Business Traveler's Guide To Fly Fishing in the Western States
Bob Zeller

A seasoned road warrior reveals where one can fly fish within a two-hour drive of every major airport in thirteen western states.
ISBN 978-1-892469-01-4 .... $18.95

Fly Fishing Central & Southeastern Oregon
Harry Teel

New waters, maps, hatch charts and illustrations. The best fly fishing in this popular region. Full color.
ISBN 978-1-892469-09-0 .... $19.95

A Woman's Guide To Fly Fishing Favorite Waters
Yvonne Graham

Forty-five of the top women fly fishing experts reveal their favorite waters. From spring creeks in the East, trout waters in the Rockies to exciting Baja—all from the female perspective.
ISBN 978-1-892469-03-8 .... $19.95

Fly Fishing Knots

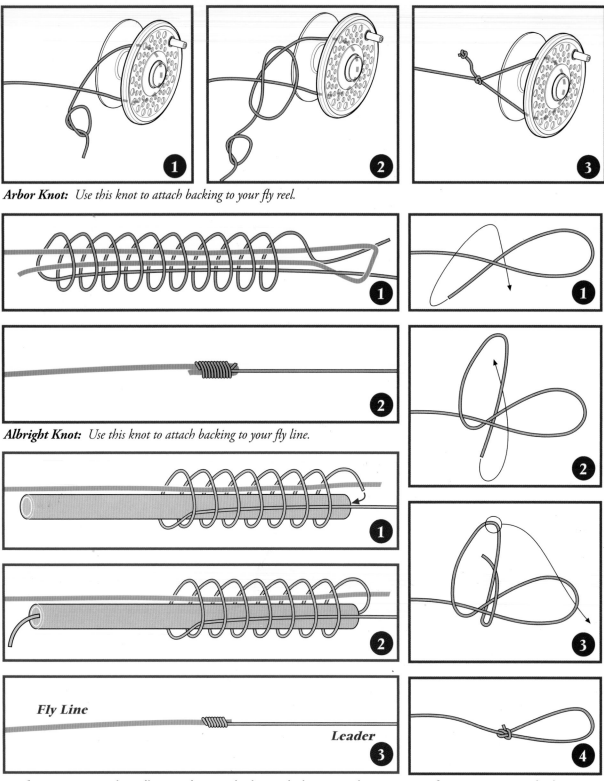

Arbor Knot: *Use this knot to attach backing to your fly reel.*

Albright Knot: *Use this knot to attach backing to your fly line.*

Fly Line

Leader

Nail Knot: *Use a nail, needle or a tube to tie this knot, which connects the forward end of the fly line to the butt end of the leader. Follow with a Perfection Loop and you've got a permanent end loop that allows easy leader changes.*

Perfection Loop: *Use this knot to create a loop in the butt end of the leader for loop-to-loop connections.*

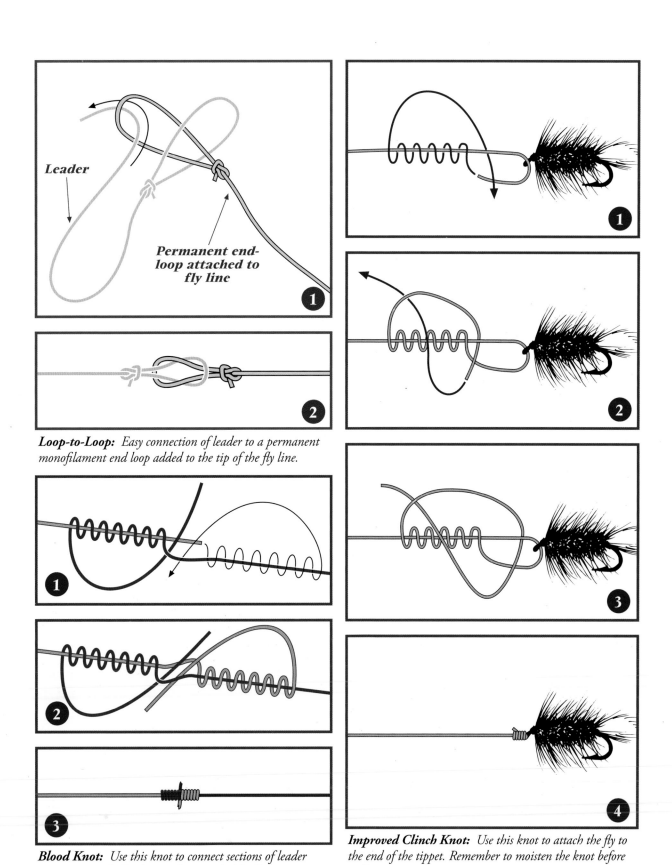

Loop-to-Loop: *Easy connection of leader to a permanent monofilament end loop added to the tip of the fly line.*

Blood Knot: *Use this knot to connect sections of leader tippet material. Hard to tie, but worth the effort.*

Improved Clinch Knot: *Use this knot to attach the fly to the end of the tippet. Remember to moisten the knot before pulling it up tight.*

Leader

Permanent end-loop attached to fly line

Carter Morris reties a fly under the falls of a small mountain creek in north Georgia.